Oxford Primary Social Studies

My Place in the World

6

Pat Lunt

OXFORD UNIVERSITY PRESS

Contents

Unit 1 Culture and identity — 3

1.1	Personal identity 1	4
1.2	Personal identity 2	6
1.3	Achieving your potential	8
1.4	Overcoming barriers	10
1.5	Socialisation	12
1.6	The wider Arab world	14
1.7	Non-Arab Muslim world 1	16
1.8	Non-Arab Muslim world 2	18
1.9	Non-Arab Muslim world 3	20
1.10	Global cultures	22
1.11	Technology and culture	24
	Review questions	26
		25

Unit 2 History and heritage

2.1	Three Muslim empires 1	28
2.2	Three Muslim empires 2	30
2.3	Three Muslim empires 3	32
2.4	A new route to India	34
2.5	World trade	36
2.6	Changing fortunes	38
2.7	18th century changes	40
2.8	Europeans in the Gulf	42
2.9	European colonial expansion	44
2.10	The results of colonisation	46
2.11	The First World War	48
2.12	After the First World War 1	50
2.13	After the First World War 2	52
2.14	Independent Arab states	54
2.15	The modern Arabian Gulf	56
2.16	Rapid development	58
	Review questions	60

Unit 3 People and places

3.1	Using maps and globes	62
3.2	Population distribution	64
3.3	World population	66
3.4	Urbanisation	68
3.5	Climate change	70
3.6	Sustainability	72
3.7	Sustainable cities	74
3.8	Deforestation	76
3.9	Trade	78
3.10	Transport connections	80
3.11	Tourism	82
	Review questions	84

Unit 4 Citizenship

4.1	Globalisation	86
4.2	Global issues 1	88
4.3	Global issues 2	90
4.4	Global issues 3	92
4.5	Poverty reduction	94
4.6	International response	96
4.7	Resources	98
4.8	Waste	100
4.9	Product life-cycles	102
4.10	The information age	104
4.11	Mass media	106
4.12	Social media	108
4.13	International relations	110
4.14	Governments and law	112
4.15	Revenue and spending	114
4.16	Democracy	116
4.17	Citizen involvement	118
4.18	Civic engagement	120
4.19	A diverse economy	122
4.20	Ethical consumers	124
4.21	Ethical products	126
	Review questions	128

Unit 5 Health and wellbeing

5.1	Progress and development	130
5.2	A healthy population	132
5.3	Globalisation and health	134
5.4	Safety on the internet	136
5.5	Dealing with change	138
	Review questions	140

Glossary — 141

1 Culture and identity

In this unit you will learn:
- about your personal identity and how to achieve your full potential in society
- about the cultures of other countries in the Arab world
- about countries in the non-Arab Muslim world and their cultures
- to understand some features of global culture, including the impact of new technologies
- to hold a class debate.

? What do you think creates a 'global culture'?

norms
stereotype   ethnic group
adolescence   official
land-locked   gender
batik

3

1.1 Personal identity 1

In this lesson you will learn:
- to identify some of the influences that help form a personal identity.

Identity and family

Our personal identity develops over time and many different factors contribute to the process. The way we think about ourselves is strongly influenced by the people with whom we have the closest relationships, especially our family. This is why good relationships within the family are so important. It is why parents should try hard to pass on to children from a young age positive values such as honesty, tolerance and respect.

Identity and gender

An individual's identity is also strongly influenced by his or her **gender**. In many societies men and women have been understood to have quite different roles and responsibilities. For example, in some traditional societies and religious groups women were understood to be responsible for managing a household and bringing up children. The role was revered and seen as having great importance. In many traditional societies it was important for the man to be the 'head of the household', to be a decision-maker and to be the main provider. Today, many of these ideas about gender are changing and it is much more common for men to be actively engaged with rearing their children and to see women in important positions such as doctors, professors, business owners and government ministers.

▲ The roles given to people of different genders are changing.

Identity and race

A person's **ethnic** background or 'race' also has an important influence on identity formation. The idea of ethnic groups may look quite simple but is really very complex. At one level it is an example of how people attempt to understand the world. We divide everything up into categories and give things a name.

Ethnic groups are, however, more than this. We may be able to identify similar physical characteristics, for example in skin colour or body shape. We may even recognise, on top of these characteristics, other distinctive cultural elements, such as language and customs. We must remember that each person within the group is an individual

This is important because, while an ethnic identity can be positive by providing a sense of identity, there can be a danger that an ethnic group is **stereotyped**. This means that all individuals in a group are assumed to have the same characteristics. Such stereotyping can mean that individuals are treated in a way that is based on their membership of the group rather than on their own personality, character or attributes. When this happens it is easy for relationships between ethnic groups to break down and to become full of distrust and hatred. Attitudes such as these can have terrible consequences such as conflict and war.

▲ These people are from different races. How much does that really tell us about them as people?

1.2 Personal identity 2

Identity and nationality

Most people understand that their **nationality** is to do with belonging to a nation. They understand that the nation they are referring to is defined by national borders.

Issues of nationality and identity have become more complex in modern times as movements of people within and between countries have increased. A result of this movement has been to see a greater mix of ethnic groups living within one country and therefore sharing the same nationality.

▲ In many societies today people from a number of different ethnic groups live together.

While it is good to feel a sense of belonging to a particular country and to experience a certain amount of pride in having a national identity, it is important to avoid this becoming a feeling of superiority, looking down on other nationals as inferior.

Identity and social groups

Outside of the family the people who have the biggest impact on us are the ones in the groups to which we belong. The closest of these groups are probably those based around friendships. As we mature and begin to recognise the things about ourselves, such as our temperament and personality, it is understandable that we seek out others who are similar. Once we identify our interests it is again understandable that we want to be with others whose interests are similar.

Identity and social institutions

Identity formation is partly achieved through understanding how we fit in to the society in which we live. The five basic social institutions that influence this process are the family, government, the economy, education and religion. These are found in one form or another in all human societies. You have seen already the important role the family has.

The government has control over how a country is ordered and how it operates.

We understand who we are as individuals partly in response to the way in which we are governed.

The economy is a system that creates employment opportunities and enables people to contribute to society. For many people their working role is an important part of their identity.

Education is one way in which knowledge, skills and attitudes are passed on from one generation to the next. As individuals within a new generation receive this input, they will be influenced in how they understand themselves.

Religion is an important part of life and acts as a guiding principle for many. In Muslim countries Islam is the focus and guide for all activities and an obviously important part of a person's identity.

▲ An important part of identity in Muslim countries is the adherence to the Islamic faith.

Activity

Write about some of the influences you think there have been on the way you understand your own identity.

1.3 Achieving your potential

In this lesson you will learn:
- to identify personal gifts, talents and abilities
- to understand the importance of setting goals
- to understand the importance of self-esteem in achieving potential.

Potential is the name given to something that has a capacity to develop into something in the future. In physics, potential energy is the energy stored inside an object such as a charged battery. The potential energy is waiting to be released and to be used.

When we apply it to a person, it usually describes qualities and abilities that are 'stored' within that person. If a person hopes to achieve their full potential, they must use their natural gifts, talents and abilities.

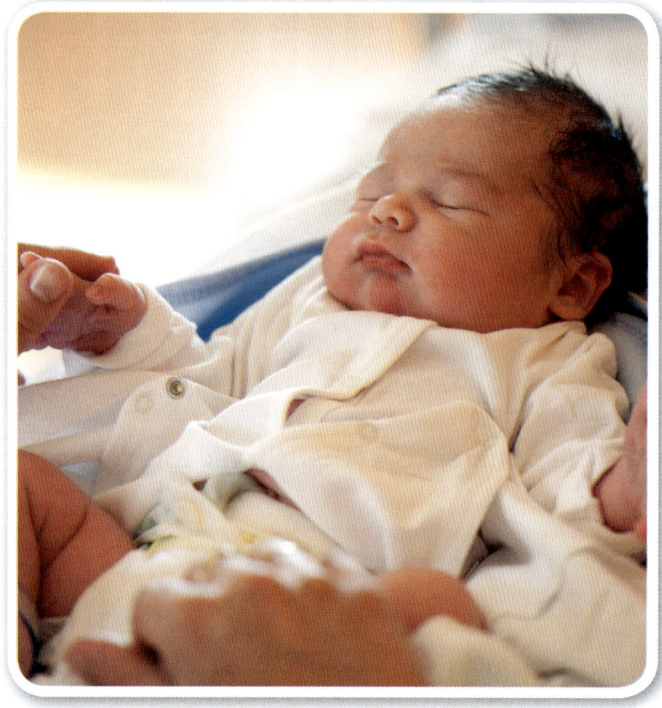

▲ A human life contains a great deal of potential.

Knowing your potential

Making the most of your potential starts with identifying the gifts, talents and abilities you possess. Some of these will become clearer as you take part in different activities such as hobbies or sports. You may find that you have certain physical and mental skills that help you to carry out your chosen activity well. Your gift may be that you can analyse a situation accurately and act quickly. You may have the ability to critically assess what a person is saying, and determine whether or not you agree with his or her views. As well as skills or talents like these you may also find you have certain qualities such as perseverance or determination that help you to keep going with tasks even when things are difficult. You may have particular gifts in terms of dealing with people which allow you to make and keep positive and strong relationships, or that help you deal with situations of conflict.

Setting goals

Setting personal goals can sometimes help in achieving potential. These can be very long-term, as in a goal of becoming a doctor, or more short-term, as in achieving good grades in an exam. Setting a long-term goal is helpful because the road to achieving that ultimate goal will be marked out with many smaller goals. Your long-term goal can motivate you to succeed in all the short-term goals along the way. The ultimate goal will also help to direct certain choices made, for example about which subjects need to be studied at different stages.

Self-esteem

To achieve your potential you need to have a strong sense of your own identity and of your value as a person. This will help you to understand that you also have a value to others and to society. You have the potential to make a contribution to creating a better and more positive world.

▲ Talent and practice are both important parts of achieving certain goals. The desire to achieve an ultimate goal can motivate us when we do not feel like putting in the practice.

Activity

Make a chart or diagram that shows the potential you have in terms of gifts, talents and abilities, the long-term and short-term goals you have and the way you feel about your ability to achieve your full potential.

1.4 Overcoming barriers

In this lesson you will learn:
- to identify barriers people can face as they try to fulfil their potential
- to identify ways in which people can overcome barriers and achieve their potential.

Did you know?
The person who holds the world record for the fastest-talking female spoke over 603 words in a minute.

There is a variety of possible barriers to achieving personal potential.

Barriers to communication

Relationships between people are at the heart of all we do and communicating is an important part of good relationships. An obvious barrier to communication is when people do not speak the same language as one another. Another example is people who find talking difficult because they lack self-confidence.

▲ There are many situations in life where people need to communicate well.

Successful communication relies as much on listening as speaking. Barriers to listening include a lack of concentration and being easily distracted. People may also listen, but not hear what is being said. They may have set ideas or prejudices which stop them from being able to receive new or different ideas.

Barriers to learning

Learning is an essential part of achieving potential. This includes the informal learning from family and friends as well as learning that takes place in formal education. Barriers to learning can include a lack of encouragement from family and friends. A person's peer group may not have a positive attitude to learning and this can influence an individual's own views.

Some people have a low opinion of themselves and do not think they have much ability. Everyone should want to achieve all that they can, regardless of what other people are capable of doing.

In some cases people face physical challenges such as poor health or a disability. A person's diet and sleep patterns can also cause problems with learning.

It is also important for people to find out how they learn best. There are three main types of learning. Visual learners do best when using objects that they can see, such as graphs and illustrations, and the written words in front of them. Auditory learners do best by speaking and listening, answering the teacher's questions, working in discussion groups. Kinaesthetic learners do best with practical activities and making things. Most people do best with a mixture of all three approaches.

Barriers to participation

People need to be able to take part in things if they are going to reach their potential. There can be barriers to participation for some people because of physical difficulties or cultural practice. There has been a great deal of improvement in recent years in helping more people participate fully in many aspects of life.

▲ In recent years, people with physical and mental impairments have been able to participate more fully in ordinary life.

Activity

Write about some of the barriers you think you face when it comes to achieving your potential and how you will overcome these.

1.5 Socialisation

In this lesson you will learn:
- to identify aspects of the process of socialisation.

Socialisation

People usually grow up in one particular culture within a certain society. Everyone needs to learn about what guides the way people live in that culture. This learning takes place through a process known as socialisation, in which **norms**, customs, ideas, values and beliefs are passed on from one generation to another.

Socialisation also teaches children about the behaviours that are acceptable in society and about the idea of negative consequences of unacceptable behaviour.

▲ All societies have special features which people need to learn about.

Families and socialisation

Most socialisation takes place in families where parents and older siblings teach young children directly about the values and ideas that are important in the family and society. Views expressed by adults and elders can have a powerful effect on the formation of an individual's own views and opinions.

Adults and older family members pass on values, attitudes and behaviours indirectly through their own behaviour. Children witnessing kindness, respect and tolerance in the interactions within a family are more likely to adopt these attitudes themselves.

Peer groups

Socialisation also happens outside the family and a particularly important influence comes from an individual's peer group. A person's peers are those who are of a similar age and social position and who share similar interests. Children in peer groups can explore their own thoughts and feelings and form relationships away from the direct influence of their parents.

Peer groups become increasingly important as children grow and reach **adolescence**. This is a period when young people are establishing their own identity. They also begin to assess their own position in relation to the adult world and their preparation for entering that world.

Schools and formal groups

Socialisation away from the home also happens in school and in other formal groups and organisations. Children learn that there may be different expectations about behaviour in various situations. This understanding is an important part of the process of maturing and becoming independent.

Religious institutions

Children learn about the role of religion in daily life from many different sources. In Muslim societies religion is at the heart of culture, and so understanding the importance of Islam in society is an important element of the process of socialisation.

▲ We learn that there are different expectations of behaviour depending on where we are.

Activity

Write about the ways in which your family, your peers and your school have helped you identify the things that are important in society and how you are expected to behave.

1.6 The wider Arab world

In this lesson you will learn:
- to identify the countries that make up the Arab world
- to identify features of the cultures of the Arab world.

> **Did you know?**
> One of the oldest mosques in Africa is the Mosque of Aqba in Tunisia, which was built in about 670CE. The current building on the site is the Great Mosque of Kairouan, built between 817 and 838CE.

▲ The countries we see on a map of the Arab world today are quite recent constructions. They have often been defined by colonial powers.

The Arab world

The Arab world stretches from the Arabian Gulf in the East to the Atlantic Ocean in the west and covers some 13.6 million square kilometres (5.25 million square miles). The population of approximately 370 million people is distributed throughout a number of countries located on the two continents of Africa and Asia.

Unity in diversity

In the Arab world there are differences in the cultures of the various lands. This diversity exists alongside the idea that the people share a common Arab identity.

The Arab conquests of Egypt and North Africa in the 7th and 8th centuries CE saw a rapid increase in Arab presence amongst the indigenous peoples. At the same time there was a widespread adoption of Islam.

North African cultures

The countries of North Africa have recognisable Arab Islamic cultures.

Arabic is the main language, alongside other national and tribal languages. In some cases a colonial language, such as French, also has an **official** status.

Clothing is similar across the region, reflecting the need to cope with the hot, dry climate and also to meet the Islamic requirements for modesty. It is usually a variation of a long, loose-fitting robe which can be worn with further shawls and cloaks. Headgear for men may be a ghutra, shmagh, turban or close-fitting cap.

North African food reflects the dietary requirements of Islam and is also influenced by local ingredients. The Mediterranean Sea provides fresh fish, and fruit and vegetables are also common. Distinctive spices are much used, often found in a special blend known as *Ras el Hanout*.

Music is usually based on a form of traditional Arab folk music with varying influences from Spanish, French and African musical forms. Forms of cultural expression such as literature and the performing and visual arts are found in varying degrees. Egypt's strong tradition of film-making began in the 1930s. There are stronger African influences on culture in Sudan.

The 'Horn of Africa'

Countries of the Arab world in the 'Horn of Africa' include Somalia, Djibouti and the island of Comoros. Languages spoken here include national languages and official languages including Arabic and, in Djibouti and Comoros, French. Clothing is similar to that found in other countries with a hot and arid climate. The rich musical heritage is based around folk music with influences from other nearby African countries and from the Arabian Peninsula. The cultures also have strong traditions of poetry, storytelling and dance. Food is often flavoured with the spices used in much other Arabic cuisine.

▲ Styles of dress across the Arab world reflect Islamic traditions and the needs of living in a hot climate.

Activity

Find out about some features of a country within the Arab world and say how this is similar or different from your own country.

1.7 Non-Arab Muslim world 1

In this lesson you will learn:
- to identify countries of the non-Arab Muslim world
- about the cultures of some of these countries.

Islam spread by a variety of means, including the conquest of neighbouring empires and territories and the expansion of trade. Several major cultures became dominant during its expansion, including Persian and Turkic, the latter being the basis for the long-lasting Ottoman Empire. As today's Muslim world contains so many different ethnic groups and indigenous cultures, it is not surprising to find a great variety of expressions of the faith in different parts of the non-Arab Muslim world today.

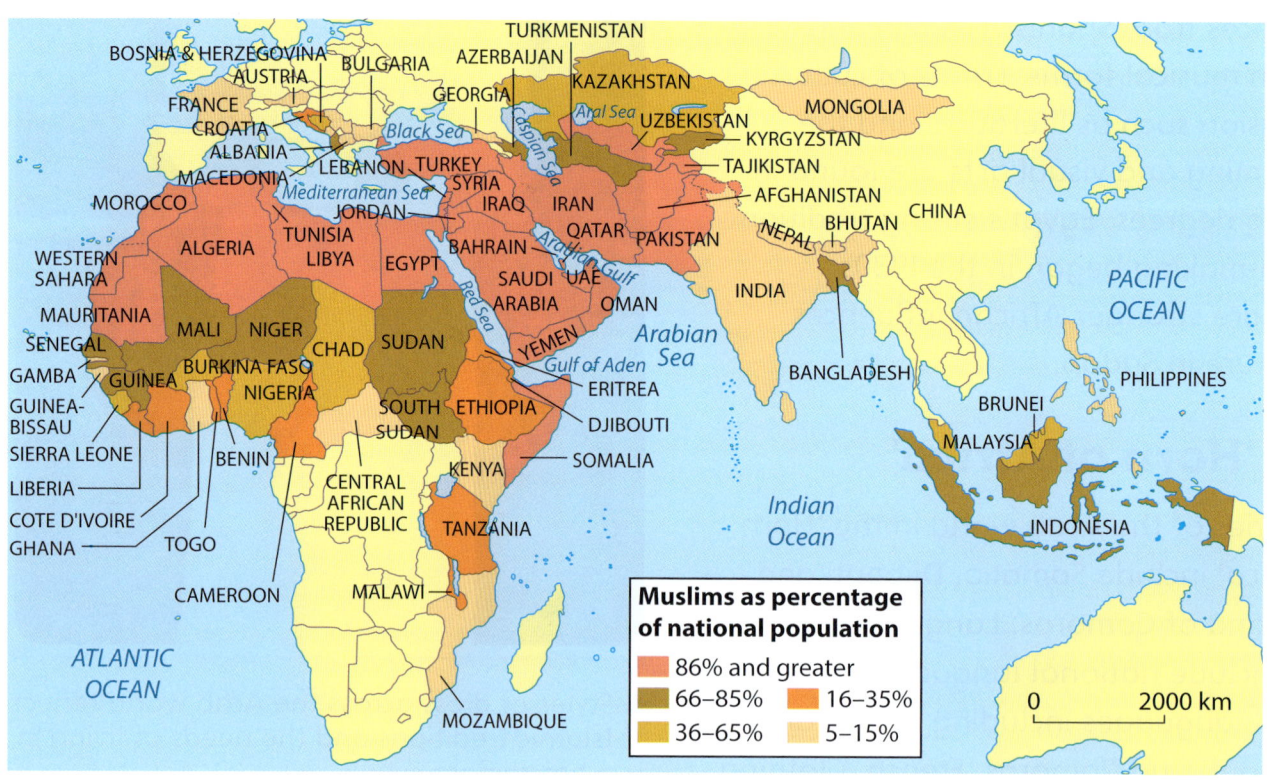

▲ The non-Arab Muslim world includes places where there are significant numbers of Muslims even though they do not make up a large part of a country's population.

West Africa

The countries of West Africa are developing nations and more than half of the populations live in simple circumstances within rural areas, often working in agricultural and craft industries. They have similar cultures, although there are many small differences due to the influences of the various ethnic groups that live within each country.

Food is based around cereal grains, sorghum and root vegetables such as yams and cassava. Rice is a staple in many countries and to these basic ingredients are added beans, peanuts, okra and vegetables. Meat, including chicken and beef, is eaten although most families will only be able to afford this occasionally. In coastal areas or in settlements on rivers or lakes, fish is an important part of the diet.

There is a strong tradition of storytelling and of keeping history alive through the use of songs and music. Traditional dances are other important features of the culture which are performed at social gatherings as well as in religious and other festivals.

Traditional dress is based around loose flowing robes which suit the hot, largely tropical climate.

◀ Mosques in non-Arab countries may look very different, as here in Burkina Faso.

Turkey

With its location at the centre of ancient trading and travelling routes between Asia and Europe, it is not surprising to learn that Turkey contains a great variety of ethnic groups and cultural influences. Classic Turkish architecture reflects a mixture of styles including Arab, Armenian, Byzantine and Persian. Great buildings from the Ottoman period include the astounding Topkapi Palace in Istanbul. Turkish cuisine is very distinctive and includes fish, stuffed and wrapped vegetables, yoghurt-based sauces and flat breads. There is a strong and varied tradition of folk music and dance.

1.8 Non-Arab Muslim world 2

South-eastern Europe

Countries in south-eastern Europe with significant Muslim populations include Albania, Bosnia-Herzegovina and Kosovo. There are many different ethnic groups in the region which has a complicated history. Some territories have known occupation at various times from Greece, Serbia, Italy and the Ottomans. This background has produced cultures that reflect these varied influences in everything from food to music and clothing.

Food is varied but largely based around local resources. Animal protein is obtained from beef, chicken, mutton and, in coastal areas, fish and seafood. Root vegetables, edible leaves and salads are common, as are olives and peppers in some areas. Dishes include pilaf, soups, stuffed vegetables and dumplings.

Popular forms of songs include folk songs, work songs, lullabies and songs of heroes and their exploits. Modern musical influences are also found, particularly in more modern, **urban areas**.

▲ Cultural heritage is important to many people and is often expressed through wearing traditional clothing. These dancers are from Croatia.

There are hundreds of variations on traditional costumes but many are based around long trousers, shirts and jackets for men and long skirts or dresses for women, often with additional shawls and scarves. Headgear includes a variety of hats, turbans and caps.

Central Asia

Countries of Central Asia in the Muslim world include Kazakhstan, Kyrgyzstan, Tajikistan, Turkmenistan and Uzbekistan. Iran, Afghanistan and Pakistan are also included here.

Many ethnic groups in the countries of Central Asia share a common heritage of nomadic herding. As a result livestock meat features in the diet and horse-riding is a common cultural element. In common with many other cultures with a nomadic heritage, the importance of hospitality and generosity towards guests is stressed.

Cuisine is based around local ingredients such as cereal grains and fruits including grapes, melons and pears. Popular dishes are soups and meat stews. Many of these countries are **land-locked** but where there is access to bodies of water, fish become a feature of the diet.

Cultural heritage is cherished and celebrated through a rich variety of forms of folk and classical music, many different types of dance and through traditional clothing.

Iran

The other major Muslim country in this region is Iran, in which the Persian culture has a strong influence on dress, architecture and art.

Afghanistan

Afghanistan is a central Asian country with borders on Pakistan, Iran, Turkmenistan, Uzbekistan, Tajikistan and China. It was formed by a collection of Pashtun tribes but is now multicultural and multi-ethnic. Afghanistan's varied landscapes allow for the production of a wide range of crops including cereals such as wheat, maize and barley and also rice and chickpeas. These are often served with vegetables and sometimes meat, especially lamb.

Pakistan

Pakistan was created in 1947 when part of India's territory was separated as part of the process which saw India gain independence from Britain. Although the present country is quite young, many of Pakistan's people are from tribes and territories whose histories go back over many centuries. These long histories are an important part of culture for many people from Pakistan. Most of the people are Muslim, so Islamic food laws are followed. Curry and spices are the main features of Pakistani cuisine, along with rice, lentils and simple breads.

1.9 Non-Arab Muslim world 3

South Asia

The South Asian countries of the Muslim world cover a wide area and once again include many different ethnic groups. There have been a number of significant cultural influences apart from Islam, including Pashtun, Turkic and Persian cultures.

These countries include Bangladesh, Bhutan, India, Maldives, Nepal and Sri Lanka.

▲ Pashtun is an ancient culture whose origins date possibly from as much as 3000 years ago.

Bangladesh

Bangladesh shares many cultural traits and similar climatic and agricultural conditions with neighbouring countries such as India. In both of these countries, approximately 77 percent of the population lives in rural areas.

South-east Asia

Between 1500 and 1800CE Islam came to be a significant influence on the peoples of the islands of South-east Asia which make up the countries known today as Indonesia, Brunei and Malaysia. As these places have been part of worldwide trade for so long, it is not surprising to find a wide range of influences on the cultures. The individual ethnic groups on the many islands have developed distinctive cultures in the past, which adds to the cultural diversity.

The environmental conditions and closeness to the sea mean that there are similarities in the ingredients found in the cuisine throughout the region. There are, however, many differences between the actual dishes created. Food is halal and based around rice, vegetables, meat and fish.

Female clothing is based around the *kebaya* which is a decorated blouse-dress combination, traditionally made of cotton, silk or lace.

Musical forms vary enormously but are largely based around percussion instruments, various forms of drum, bamboo flutes and a number of stringed instruments.

There are strong artistic traditions of stone sculpting and painting as well as applying designs to textiles using techniques such as **batik.**

East Asia

There are estimated to be over 21 million Muslims in China but because the total population is over 1.3 billion people this represents only one to two percent. The highest concentrations are in the north-western provinces of Xinjiang, Gansu and Ningxia, areas that are close to the borders with Central Asia.

▲ Some mosques in China are based on traditional Chinese architecture while others have features more familiar from Asian examples, such as domes and minarets.

Activity

Work in a group to identify some aspects of the culture of a non-Arab Muslim country.

1.10 Global cultures

In this lesson you will learn:
- to understand how cultural ideas spread
- to identify the influences of global culture
- to describe some of the effects of the influences of global culture.

Cultural exchange and communication

The spread of cultural ideas has always been closely tied to the development of transport and communication because these are the things that allow people from different cultures to meet and share their thoughts and experiences. As the means of transportation and communication improved, new ideas spread more quickly and travelled further.

The extensive road networks created by the Persians in the 5th and 6th centuries BCE, and later by the Romans, show the effect of such changes in transportation. Communication helped create these empires and then allowed their culture to influence territories across large areas of the world.

As shipbuilding and navigation improved and allowed for safer journeys over greater distances, so ideas from even more widely separated cultures were exchanged. The speed of transportation methods increased with railways and motor vehicles. The invention of the telegraph in the 19th century introduced almost instantaneous communication across long distances. Today there is a global network of computers and telecommunications devices that allow for information to be instantly available around the globe.

▲ Technological advances in air travel have had a huge impact on the way people and goods travel.

Impacts of global cultural exchange

The spread of cultural ideas in the past occurred through conquest and colonisation, or as a result of relationships formed around trade and commerce. The way cultural ideas spread today is very different and their area of influence is now truly global.

Much cultural influence today is passed on through media such as television and the internet. In some respects this huge exchange of ideas is to be welcomed.

People around the world can connect in new ways and create new social networks. This can help people from different groups understand one another. Positive ideas such as universal human rights can spread, along with global values that drive the ideals of ending poverty and preventable childhood deaths and ensuring that everyone receives a primary education.

For some people, however, there are negative aspects to this global reach. Part of this reaction is because of some unwelcome elements of the dominant global cultures. There are also concerns that a dominant global culture could overwhelm local cultures and so lead people to lose their unique cultural identity.

Cultural penetration

Cultural penetration is a phrase used to describe the way in which aspects of one culture are introduced and promoted into another culture. Cultural penetration can be brought about through the introduction of certain types of diet, particular foods, language, music or styles of clothing. An entire cultural lifestyle can be promoted through mass media and movies.

◀ Satellite communications and other communications technologies allow for transmission of ideas with no regard for national boundaries.

Activity

Hold a debate about the importance of preserving local cultural traditions.

1.11 Technology and culture

In this lesson you will learn:
- to identify new technologies
- to identify and evaluate the impact of these new technologies on culture.

Technology and culture

Technology is a means by which people try to provide for their needs and for their enjoyment.

Technology always develops within the context of a human culture and it is intimately connected with people and their wants and needs. This means that the products of technology can reflect ideas and values from within a culture. At the same time, the technological products and innovations can influence the values and ideas within a culture.

One illustration of this is the printing press. A printing press with a moveable type system was invented in the middle of the 15th century in response to greater demand for written records. The device created in response to demands from a culture was used to spread new ideas in science, technology and learning and to bring about cultural changes.

Industrialisation

Industrialisation is a process in which the general pattern of employment in a country changes from one where most people work in agriculture to one where most people work in industry. As industries are usually based in urban areas, the pattern of population distribution also changes, with increasing numbers of people living in towns and cities and fewer living in the countryside.

Many countries in Europe, together with North America and Japan, became industrialised in the 19th century. More countries became industrialised during the 20th century.

The impact of new technologies

The introduction of a new technology can have many effects beyond the actual activity in which the technology is used.

For example, the invention of the animal-drawn plough in ancient times would certainly have made the job of ploughing a field a great deal easier. However, it would also have brought greater areas of land under cultivation, leading to an increase in food production. A larger population could be supported and excess food traded with other societies, leading to the exchange of goods and also of ideas and technology.

◀ What impact might solar panels have in a remote village in the developing world?

Did you know?
The World Bank estimates that 1.2 billion people on the planet (about 20 percent of the global population) do not have access to electricity, with about 550 million of these people living in Africa and over 400 million in India.

Technologies today

Technological change and innovation occurs faster than ever today. The area that has seen the most significant change, and therefore had the greatest impact, has been communication. This has never been so easy, fast and widespread.

Communications technology has transformed the way in which people find information, buy and sell goods and services and communicate with one another. The world is more open and possibilities for sharing knowledge and mutual understanding have increased.

▲ Many people today are constantly 'connected' to the internet and the World Wide Web.

Activity

Work in a group to discuss how modern technologies might change traditional cultures and how they could be used to promote aspects of traditional culture and prevent these from disappearing.

Unit 1 Review questions

1. When a person is a citizen of a particular country this is known as their:
   a culture
   b nationality
   c custom
   d heritage

2. The process by which people are taught the customs, values, ideas and beliefs of the society in which they grow up, is called:
   a socialisation
   b indoctrination
   c preparation
   d immunisation

3. When a language has a legal status in a country it is called an:
   a accepted language
   b original language
   c official language
   d indigenous language

4. When a set of characteristics are applied to all individual members of a group, this is known as:
   a discrimination
   b stereotyping
   c prejudice
   d inequality

5. Which of the following are important parts of oral history?
   a Food and drink
   b Traditional clothing
   c Storytelling and songs
   d Traditional dances

6. Two countries of the Arab world on the African continent are:
   a Sudan and Bangladesh
   b Egypt and Uzbekistan
   c Iraq and Algeria
   d Somalia and Libya

7. People from different cultures wear traditional dress mostly to:
   a celebrate their culture and heritage
   b take part in costume parades
   c practise their sewing skills
   d engage in sporting events

8. Identify two sources of influence on an individual's personal identity and describe what the effect of these influences might be.

9. Write about some similarities and differences amongst the cultures of the countries of the Arab World and explain why these exist.

10. Write a brief explanation of why some people might feel that maintaining aspects of traditional cultures is important. Say how food, clothes and music are important in achieving this.

11. Explain how new technologies have increased cultural exchange and describe some of the effects of these exchanges.

2 History and heritage

In this unit you will learn:
- about the empires of the early Muslim world
- about the importance of trade
- about changes in the Arabian peninsula from the 18th to the 21st centuries
- to create timelines for events in the past.

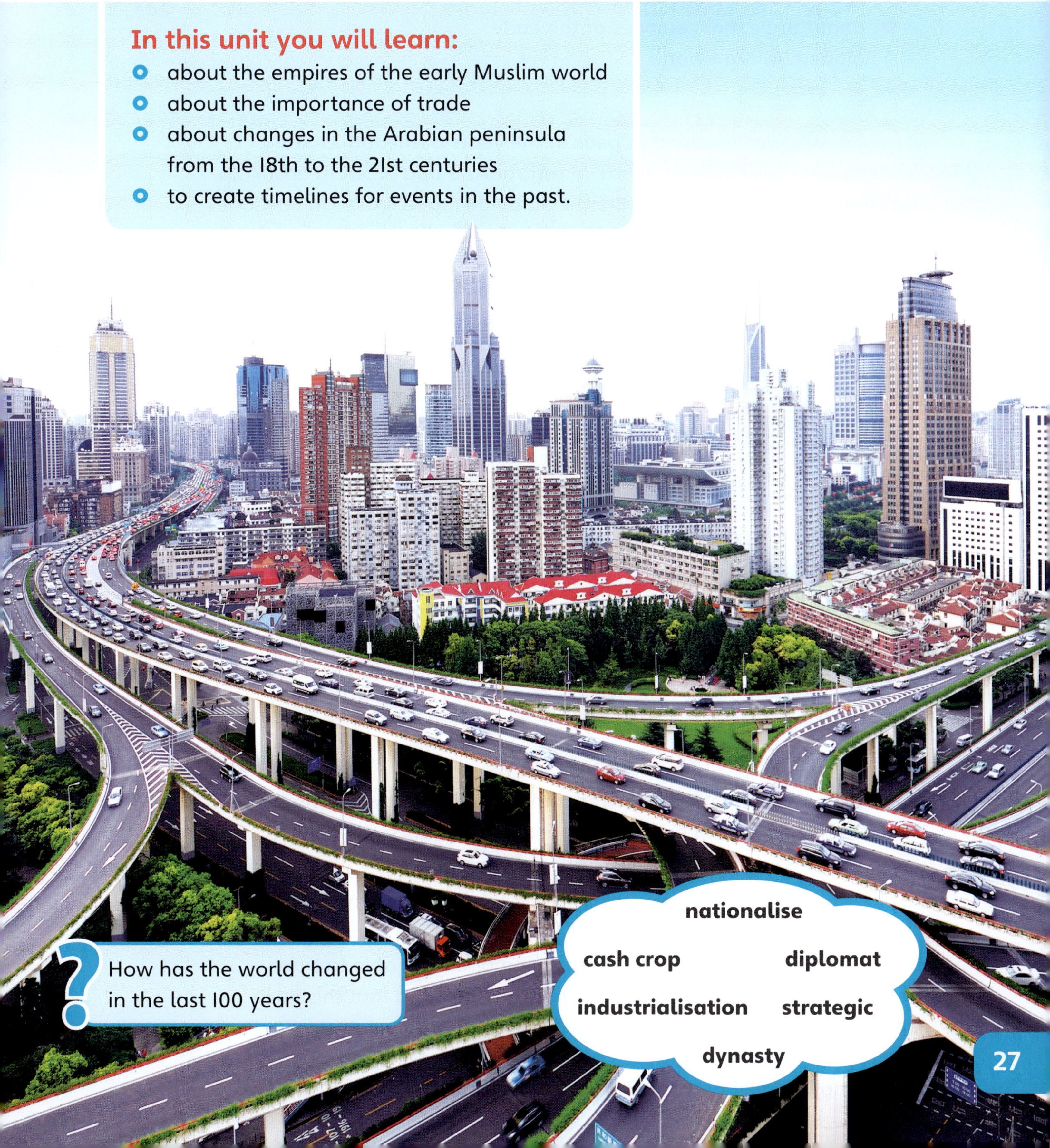

? How has the world changed in the last 100 years?

nationalise

cash crop   diplomat

industrialisation   strategic

dynasty

2.1 Three Muslim empires 1

In this lesson you will learn:
- about three main empires of the early modern Muslim world.

Muslim power was reaching its peak in the years of the 16th century CE. New empires arose in West Africa, in central Asia and in South-east Asia. The strongest empires by far were the Safavid Empire, based in territories of modern day Iran, the Mughal Empire in India and the Ottoman Empire which covered lands in south-eastern Europe, the Middle East and North Africa. Although all these empires were Islamic, culture was expressed differently in each one.

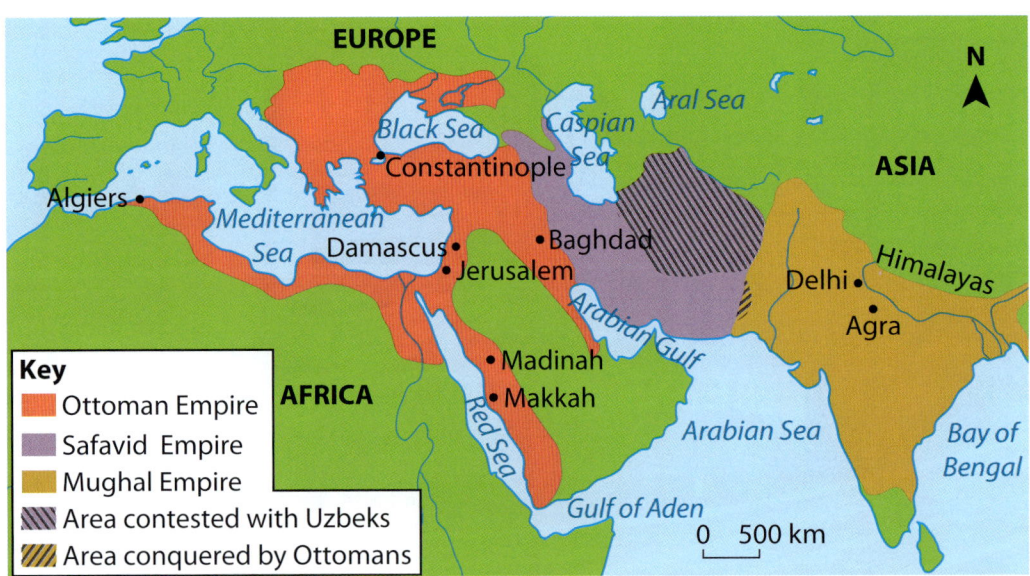

▲ The Ottoman, Safavid and Mughal Empires.

These states are sometimes referred to as the Gunpowder Empires, because they each used newly developed firearms such as cannons and handguns to help in their military campaigns. Having these weapons meant the empires' forces would be more likely to beat other armies who were not so well armed.

The ruling families or **dynasties** of each empire were able to trace their ancestors a long way back in time. They believed that this gave them a strong right to be rulers in the eyes of their populations. To maintain control over vast areas of land, each ruler understood the need to have a well-organised system of government. To feed a large and growing population they also needed an efficient system of agricultural production. All these empires became centres of Islamic cultural achievement.

The Safavid Empire

The first Safavids are thought to have been sufi sheiks whose religious order was founded by Safi al-Din (1252–1334CE). The Safavid order adopted Shi'ism and transformed into a revolutionary movement that would fight for its beliefs. The Safavid Empire was founded by Shah Ismail I in 1501CE when he was just 14 years old. In his early years as ruler Ismail focused on bringing together the different Iranian tribes to create a unified state. He had largely succeeded in this by 1507. In 1508 the Safavids moved westwards into the eastern 'Fertile Crescent' area of Mesopotamia, taking many cities, including Baghdad.

The Safavids took territories from the Uzbek people of Central Asia after a major battle in 1510. Despite this defeat, the Uzbeks fought to regain this land for the rest of the century.

Safavid expansion to the west brought them into conflict with the Ottomans who held those lands at that time. There was a decisive battle in 1514 on the plains of Chaldiran, in which the Safavids were defeated. The Ottomans had more fighters and were using better weapons, such as cannons and muskets. These military advantages allowed the Ottomans steadily to take more lands. Shah Ismail died in 1524 at the age of 37.

▲ Shah Ismail I at the Battle of Chaldiran

2.2 Three Muslim empires 2

Further Safavid expansion

Shah Ismail's descendants concentrated on expanding Safavid territories to the east and brought tighter controls over tribal leaders. When Shah Abbas became ruler in 1587CE he reorganised the structure of government and made the empire more unified and secure. By 1606 he had been successful in military campaigns against both the Ottomans and the Uzbeks. This reduced the threat of attack from both these groups and led to a period of security, stability and peace during which many other achievements were made.

By creating a peaceful countryside, Shah Abbas oversaw an increase in agricultural production. This would reduce the threat of food shortages and possibly allow for some trade. He also encouraged industries to develop, especially the manufacture of carpets and silk products. He welcomed traders and ambassadors from Europe and oversaw the flourishing of Persian art and architecture.

Shah Abbas made the city of Isfahan his capital. This grew to be one of the largest cities of its time, with a population of about 1 million, and one of the most beautiful of all time. The main feature was *al Maiden*, a large area which included tiers of shops, a palace and splendid mosques.

The Safavid Empire finally ended in 1760CE.

◀ Minarets of the Imam mosque built by Shah Abbas.

The Mughal Empire

The Mughal Empire was founded by Zahir-ud-din Babur, in 1526CE. He was descended through his father from Timur, a Muslim warrior who had founded his own empire in the late 1300s CE. Through his mother he was descended from Genghis Khan, the mighty leader and founder of the Mongol Empire in the early 1200s CE.

Babur's son, Humayun, ruled the empire next (1530–1540 and 1555–1556). He was followed by his son Akbar who became ruler in 1556CE.

At this time a period of Mughal greatness began. Territories were slowly conquered and brought within the empire. Capturing territories on the coast allowed the Mughals to trade with countries across the Indian Ocean. Before this they had needed to trade across land held by other empires. Akbar created large and effective military forces and also developed the government systems. These two things made the empire strong and ensured that it would last a long time.

Money collected from the large population was used to run the government, pay the standing armies and provide funds for a large building programme. Great cities were built and many great garden tombs, the most famous of which is perhaps the Taj Mahal in India.

▲ Which features of this Mughal building in India suggest Islamic influences in the architecture?

2.3 Three Muslim empires 3

Unlike the Safavid and Ottoman Empires, the Mughal Empire was founded in a society where most of the population were not Muslims. As a result, art and architecture show influences of both Islamic and Indian traditions.

The last 'Great Mughal' was Awrangzeb, who ruled from 1658 to 1707CE.

The Ottoman Empire

The Ottoman Empire was founded by Osman I in 1299CE. It became the strongest of the three great Muslim empires of the central Islamic world and the one that would last for the longest period of time. By 1500CE the Ottoman state was becoming one of the most powerful in the world.

> **Did you know?**
> At their greatest extent, the Safavid, Mughal and Ottoman Empires had a combined area of approximately 13 million square kilometres, which was almost 8 percent of the total land area of the world.

In 1453CE the Ottomans had succeeded in taking the city of Constantinople, the capital of the Byzantine Empire. This was an important victory for the Muslim forces which allowed successive Ottoman rulers to take greater control over more territory. The **strategic** lands that were of most interest were those offering the chance of more control over world trade.

Selim I was sultan from 1512 to 1520CE and his rule was marked by a period of rapid expansion. Lands were taken along the eastern Mediterranean, in Egypt, where Selim overthrew the Mamluk Sultanate, and in the Arabian Peninsula. Selim now controlled the two cities of Makkah and Madinah and was given the title of 'The Servant of the Two Holy Shrines'. His successor was Suleiman the Magnificent who ruled from 1520 to 1566CE. This period saw a further expansion of territories along the coast of North Africa and into the heartlands of Europe.

After this period of expansion came the reign of Selim II, which lasted from 1566 to 1574CE. During this time the Ottomans concentrated on defending their borders and recapturing any territories they had previously lost.

▲ Osman I, founder of the Ottoman Empire.

Ottoman culture was expressed in many ways. As in most Islamic states, poetry was of great importance but so too were biographies and also travel writing. Euliya Chelebi (1614–1682CE) spent 40 years travelling throughout the Ottoman lands and recorded his experiences in ten volumes of writings called *A Book of Travels*. There were great advances in the production of carpets, textiles and ceramics, but architecture is perhaps the best expression of Ottoman cultural achievement. Many gardens, tombs, palaces and magnificent mosques were built. The works of the royal architect Sinan include the Selimiye mosque, built in Edirne between 1569 and 1575CE.

▲ The Topkapi Palace in Istanbul was the main residence of the Ottoman sultans for 400 years.

Activities

1 Create a timeline for each of the three early Muslim empires.

2 Write about two significant events or achievements during the time of these empires. Illustrate your work with a drawing.

2.4 A new route to India

In this lesson you will learn:
- to identify the importance of established trade routes for traders in the Arabian Peninsula
- to explain why traders from other nations were searching for another route
- to describe how a new trading route between Europe and India was established.

Established trade routes

The different Muslim empires all needed wealth. Much of this came from the trade in goods between the countries of the Far East and South-east Asia and the markets of Europe. Trading created profits but the governments also applied taxes and **duties** to the goods.

The long-established trade routes included the overland Silk Road and the sea-going Spice Routes. Almost all the routes ended at the ports on the eastern Mediterranean.

As a result, the trade with Europe was almost exclusively in the hands of Arab traders. They wanted to keep secret the original source of the special luxury goods from the East.

By the time these goods reached their final destination they had passed through many traders. Each trader made a profit and so the goods became very expensive. Anyone who could find an alternative route to Asia which allowed for goods to be transported in one journey would make a much greater profit for themselves.

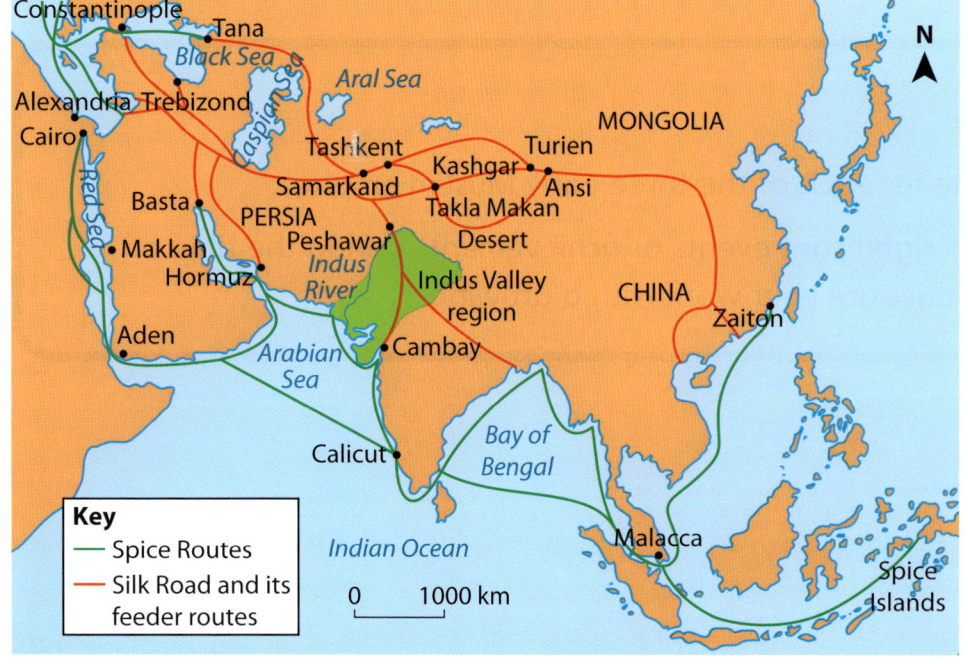

The Silk Road and Spice Routes were well established and gave much control over trade to those in and around the Arabian Peninsula.

Searching for a new route

In the 15th century there were several barriers to exploration and finding new trade routes. There were still no reliable maps that showed the whole of the world. Some people still believed that the Earth was flat.

Most intelligent people, however, knew the world to be round. In Europe, people had the idea that if they sailed far enough west, they would eventually reach lands in the east. The lands they eventually hoped to reach were the wealth-producing Spice Islands.

By sailing west across the Atlantic, Europeans found the American continents and began colonising. The Portuguese were also exploring down the west coast of Africa. In 1488 an explorer called Bartholomew Dias sailed around the southern tip of Africa (later named the Cape of Good Hope) and opened the possibility of exploring further. Ten years later Vasco da Gama, another Portuguese explorer, followed the route around the Cape and then sailed further on. As da Gama's ships came to ports further north they encountered traders from India. Eventually da Gama discovered what Arabian sailors knew about the winds that blew across the Indian Ocean. This allowed him to sail his expedition across the Indian Ocean. In this way a new sea route between Europe and India was opened.

The route established by Vasco da Gama was long, difficult and dangerous. The Portuguese knew they would need supply points and that their shipping could be vulnerable to attack. To meet these challenges they determined to take control of strategic points around the Arabian Peninsula.

▲ The route of Vasco da Gama's first journey.

Did you know?

Vasco da Gama left India as the monsoon season started and encountered terrible storms. It took the ships three months to sail across the Indian Ocean instead of three weeks and it took a whole year for them to return to Portugal.

Activity

Write a brief report describing how the new trade route around Africa was discovered. Include in your answer the effects it could have had on traders who used the traditional routes.

2.5 World trade

In this lesson you will learn:
- to describe the struggles for control of trade routes
- to describe some of the relationships between Muslim powers and European nations.

The Portuguese in the Arabian Peninsula

The Portuguese had established a new trading route to India. Now they wanted to secure it, to protect their shipping, to create supply points and to limit Arab activity. A man called Alfonso de Albuquerque was given the task of capturing suitable places to achieve these aims.

One such place was the town of Hormuz on an island in the Arabian Gulf, which had a commanding position over the Straits of Hormuz. Albuquerque took the town in 1507 and made it a **tributary state**. The following year the sultanate of Hormuz revolted and retook the town which regained its independence.

In 1515 Albuquerque assaulted Aden, in present-day Yemen, in order to control the Red Sea routes. The attempt failed and he returned to retake Hormuz. With Hormuz taken, many other ports on the Arabian side of the Gulf fell under Portuguese control. Various rebellions were put down throughout the 1500s and the Portuguese used their positions to launch raids on other shipping in the area.

▲ Julfar was one of the ports that fell under Portuguese control.

The Ottomans respond

Portugal's main rivals for control of trade were the Ottomans. The Ottomans also had rivals in the Mamluk dynasty that ruled Egypt. The Ottomans overthrew the Mamluks in Egypt in 1517 and gained control of the trade route up the Red Sea. They later expanded their control of territories in the Arabian Peninsula around the holy cities of Makkah and Madinah.

The Portuguese took Al Qatif, in present-day Saudi Arabia, from the Ottomans in 1551, while the Ottomans attacked Portuguese strongholds in Bahrain and Muscat. The Ottoman Empire and the Portuguese Empire were engaged in many years of conflict, often involving naval battles in the Indian Ocean, as each tried to establish control of the spice trade. There was a Portuguese presence in the Arabian Gulf and Peninsula until they were finally expelled in the middle of the 1600s.

Ottoman relations with Europe

At the beginning of the 1600s, the Ottoman Empire was still the wealthiest and most powerful state in the world. The relationship of the Ottoman Empire with a number of European countries was frequently marked by conflict. This was largely over control of trade routes, especially those in the eastern Mediterranean and the Indian Ocean. Despite this, trading relationships had to be maintained, since this was the source of much of the Ottoman Empire's wealth.

◀ Enamelled glassware was imported into Europe from the 1200s CE. By the middle of the 1500s, lamps of fine Venetian glass were being ordered for use as mosque lamps.

Activity

Work in a group to establish where Portuguese forts and settlements are located in the Arabian Gulf and other parts of the Arabian Peninsula. Suggest why these locations were chosen.

2.6 Changing fortunes

In this lesson you will learn:
- to describe how global power shifted towards Europe in the 18th century.

Throughout the 1600s the three great Muslim empires had continued to grow in strength and influence. In the 18th century there were great changes in their fortunes and each one, in different ways and at different rates, began to decline.

In Europe at that time, competition among the stronger countries, including the Dutch, French, Spanish, English and Portuguese, grew stronger. This competition was mostly centred on the trade in spices and other exotic goods from India and South-east Asia. European countries in the 1600s also began to devote more of their attention to the 'New Worlds' of North and South America. Resources from these territories provided new wealth which allowed for great progress in culture, science and technology.

▲ A turning point for Ottoman fortunes was their defeat at the Siege of Vienna in 1683, which marked the end of their expansion into new territories.

Change in Europe

European and Ottoman power remained in balance until the middle of the 18th century. In the last quarter of that century some countries of western and northern Europe saw important changes in industry, agriculture, medicine and military weapons. All of these combined to give them advantages over many countries in other parts of the world.

In industry there were new methods of manufacturing which kept **production costs** low and allowed for goods to be produced on a massive scale. All this meant that the finished goods were cheaper than most others of similar quality from anywhere in the world. People would therefore buy these goods wherever they were available. Years of exploration had refined European shipbuilding techniques and navigation methods. This meant they could obtain resources from all over the world while taking manufactured goods to these new markets.

Advances in medical understanding and treatment in Europe helped to control illness. Some terrible diseases had previously killed large numbers of people and the smaller populations made European countries weaker. This was no longer the case and illnesses were more contained and did far less damage.

A problem always associated with a growing population is feeding all the people. Before this time there had been many famines but new ideas in agriculture meant that production was high enough to prevent this.

▲ New agricultural machines improved efficiency and increased production in Europe. This seed drill, perfected in 1701, economically sowed seeds in neat rows.

Having fought so many wars amongst themselves, the European countries had developed their military technology to the point where they had some of the most advanced weapons available.

All of these factors gave the European nations a strong position as they entered the 1800s and the period of colonisation.

Activity

Work in a group to make a presentation that explains some of the advantages the European countries developed in the later 1700s.

2.7 18th century changes

In this lesson you will learn:
- to identify changes in the organisation and settlement of peoples in the Arabian peninsula in the 18th century.

At the start of the 18th century, societies within the Arabian Peninsula were still organised around tribal societies whose people occupied territories that were not fixed. People lived mainly in three distinct situations: coastal settlements, oasis settlements and the desert.

Some of those in the coastal settlements made their living from the sea, as fishermen or in the pearl diving industry. Others engaged in trade which took place up and down the Gulf as goods passed through the region between India and the markets of Europe. Fishing, pearl diving and trade all relied on boats. For many people, another way of making a living was to build boats.

The oasis settlements were based around those areas where sufficient water could be found for people and animals, and for a range of permanent vegetation. The most important plant was the date palm which provided food and also materials for buildings, making brushes and basket-weaving. Some cereal crops would also have been grown, with any surplus being traded in the coastal towns.

The desert was the domain of the Bedouin people, who raised livestock, usually camels or goats, and moved with their animals across large areas in search of pasture and water.

The situation in the Arabian Peninsula in the 18th century was affected by developments

◀ People in many coastal settlements were involved in the pearl diving industry, an important source of income.

in other parts of the world. The modern countries of Europe as we know them today had been changing during the previous century. The way those countries related to one another and to other countries around the world was also changing. They were becoming used to dealing with one another as nations rather than simply as groups of people.

During the 18th century, local Arab rulers came to see that they too would need to make some changes if they were to take full advantage of the international trade that was taking place in different parts of the world. This was especially important because a large amount of that trade passed through Arabian waters and across Arabian lands.

During the century there was a wave of tribal movements that saw many people moving to, and settling along, the coast. For example, the Qawasim settled in the area of Ras al Khaimah and Sharjah during this time. The Bani Yas spread out from their established territories around the Liwa oasis to settle in the area around Abu Dhabi. The Al Khalifah occupied Bahrain for the first time in 1701 and they were well established by the 1780s. In Kuwait, the al Sabah established themselves in 1720 and in 1752 elected their first emir, who founded Kuwait as an entity.

◀ The nomadic Bedouin were always an important part of societies in the Arabian Gulf region.

Activity

Write a brief explanation of the way in which the resources available in different places, and the development of trade, may have affected settlement patterns in the Arabian Gulf during the 18th century.

2.8 Europeans in the Gulf

In this lesson you will learn:
- to describe early European involvement in the Arabian Gulf.

Early European involvement

Throughout the 1600s and 1700s, European presence in the region was largely motivated by a desire to secure trade and trading routes.

The Portuguese were finally removed by Omani forces from Hormuz in 1622, from Julfar in 1633 and from Muscat in 1650. During the period between 1600 and 1664 some special trading companies called 'East India Companies' were founded in England, Holland and France.

▲ There was a huge market in Europe for tea. This was grown in countries of South Asia such as India.

These companies grew to be powerful and to have great influence. They acted almost as if they were nations in themselves, and even had their own armies. There was intense rivalry between them. In the 1600s each one was trying hard to make special trading arrangements with rulers and tribal leaders on both sides of the Arabian Gulf.

European involvement in the early 1800s

The intentions of the Europeans changed in 1798 when the French, under the command of Napoleon I, attempted to colonise Egypt. If he succeeded, the resources of Egypt, including the highly valued cotton, would become available to France and Napoleon would gain important ports on the Mediterranean and the Red Sea.

▲ Cotton was a valuable resource used in the large textile industries of Europe.

The British saw this as a threat to their dominant position over trade in the region and formed an alliance with the Ottoman Empire. The Ottomans still officially ruled Egypt although it was largely under the control of Mamluk rulers. The British Navy defeated the French fleet while the Ottoman army fought the French on land. The French finally surrendered in 1801 and Egypt remained within the Ottoman Empire under Mamluk rule.

Later, when the Egyptian and Ottoman forces defeated the first attempt to form a Saudi state in 1818, the British again saw this as a threat to their trade routes. They began to strengthen their position in other parts of the region. In the Arabian Gulf, they claimed that their trading ships were often raided by boats coming from local ports. In response to these raids they attacked several places along the coast. In 1820 they brought the sheiks of these different areas together to sign the first in a series of peace treaties. This was the beginning of British dealings with what they called the 'Trucial Sheikdoms' or 'Trucial States'.

Aden, in southern Yemen, was an important port near the entrance to the Red Sea. Its position meant it had great strategic value as a supply port. The British also felt it was a source of possible attacks on their shipping. For these reasons, forces from the British East India Company occupied the port of Aden in 1839.

▲ What is the strategic importance of the places shown on this map?

Activity

Using the information in this lesson and further research, make a timeline of European involvement in the Arabian Peninsula from the 1500s to 1850.

Did you know?

An agreement between enemies or opponents who agree to stop fighting for a certain time is called a truce. This is why the British called the sheikdoms that agreed to stop fighting, the Trucial States.

2.9 European colonial expansion

In this lesson you will learn:
- to describe reasons for European colonial expansion.

During the 19th century European countries came to dominate the world. A number of factors are thought to be behind the huge European expansion during this period.

The need for more resources

During this period many European countries were experiencing a period of industrialisation. This process saw a number of new inventions and industrial processes that made it possible to produce goods rapidly on a very large scale. This huge increase in the rate and speed of production meant that there was a much greater demand for resources. To keep up with their rivals each country needed to keep the factories running. To access the resources to achieve this, the countries set about taking control of the territories where these resources were found. These territories also provided new markets for the goods being produced.

The need for new resources

Many new materials were being discovered and their uses explored. Many of these resources, such as oil, rubber and certain metals, were not available in Europe, and so they had to be obtained from abroad.

▲ Rubber is made from the sap from certain types of trees that only grow in tropical climates. Inventors were finding many uses for rubber in the 19th century, including waterproof clothing and bicycle tyres.

Strategic positions

Lands were sometimes occupied for strategic reasons. In a time before air travel, the fact that one country bordered another one was very significant. Countries acted as buffers between the neighbouring countries on either side. Some colonies were occupied by one nation to prevent a rival nation spreading too far. Other lands were occupied because they were in a good position to offer protection or control of trading routes.

Local unrest

In countries like Egypt, colonisation had complicated causes. After the French defeat in 1801, Muhammad Ali had declared himself as ruler. He introduced some modernising reforms which increased production in agriculture, industry and trade. He drove out the British in 1807 but they returned in 1881 to help suppress a popular uprising. This was a protest about the extent of European influence being allowed by the ruling dynasty. This dynasty was restored to power, but the occupation by British military forces continued.

European colonialism in the Middle East and North Africa

There had been a European presence in the Arabian Gulf region since the Portuguese had arrived in 1515, but it was in the 19th century that other countries of the Arab Muslim world fell under European control in a new way. The first major conquest of an Arabic-speaking country was that of Algeria in 1830. Over the course of the century different European countries colonised many of the countries of North Africa and the Middle East, and elsewhere around the world.

◀ A major cause of European concern over Egypt was the Suez Canal, an important waterway linking the Mediterranean and the Red Sea which had been completed in 1869. What significance would this canal have for Britain or France?

Activity

Prepare a short report that explains some of the reasons behind the European colonisation of different places, including countries in North Africa and the Middle East.

2.10 The results of colonisation

In this lesson you will learn:
- to identify and describe some of the consequences of European colonisation.

Colonisation had a wide range of effects on the different countries under European control.

Loss of independence

The immediate effect of a country being colonised is the loss of independence and freedom to govern.

The degree of control a colonising power had was not always the same. In some cases, as with the 'Trucial States', the countries became a 'protectorate' of the colonising power. In this situation, local rulers still ruled within their lands while the colonising power offered military protection. In return for this protection, the rulers made special agreements to do with trade and foreign policy.

Trade and development

Trade within an empire usually involved finished goods being sent out to the colonies and resources being sent back to the industries of the colonial power.

◀ A busy scene in Algiers in 1894CE.

For some people involved in a traditional industry, such as hand-woven textiles or small-scale pottery, the arrival of cheap, mass-produced goods from the industrialised nations was not good. If they could not compete they would be put out of business.

Trade in food helped the colonial powers who were often struggling to feed their large populations. New agricultural practices introduced in the colonies meant that food production increased. The local populations had enough to eat and the food surplus was exported.

These new agricultural techniques and practices did sometimes cause problems. Many people in the colonised territories were small-scale subsistence farmers whose way of life was completely disrupted, and even ruined, if they lost ownership of their land. Sometimes too much land was given over to growing **cash crops** produced for export rather than growing food for the local population.

▲ Egypt was one of the first non-European countries to experience people travelling as tourists.

The colonised countries also experienced some development. Communications would be improved by the construction of railways, improved roads and telegraph systems. Machinery and tools would be sent out to make these improvements possible and to allow for the manufacture of some goods.

Government

Some ideas about ways of governing were retained by countries that had been colonised after they gained their independence.

Culture and education

Colonising powers would often introduce ideas and values from their own cultures which were not always welcomed by the local populations. In some cases reforms were introduced to education systems. These often only helped richer people. They were partly to ensure that there would be people who could work on behalf of the colonising power.

Activity

Carry out research into a country in the Middle East or North Africa that was colonised by a European power. Find out what form of colonisation took place, what goods were traded between the two countries and the cultural influence of the colonial power.

2.11 The First World War

In this lesson you will learn:
- to identify some causes of the First World War
- to consider why Arab forces became involved in the First World War.

The outbreak of the First World War

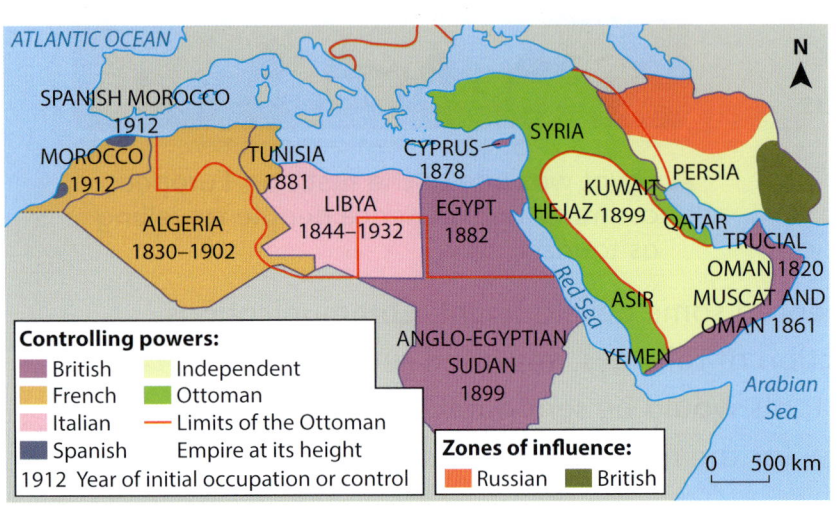

The different controlling powers in the Middle East in 1914CE.

There was no single cause for the First World War, but a number of different factors came together. European powers were all still competing to be powerful forces in the world. Countries also made special agreements or 'alliances' between themselves about what one would do if the other was attacked.

In 1914, Austria controlled the country of Bosnia. Archduke Franz Ferdinand was the heir to the Austria-Hungarian throne. He was visiting Bosnia in June 1914 when he was shot by a Serbian who thought that Serbia should have control of Bosnia. Following this event Austria-Hungary declared war on Serbia.

Due to their special agreements several countries, including Russia, France, Belgium and Britain, joined forces against Austria-Hungary. Germany fought with Austria-Hungary and these countries were later joined by the Ottoman Empire.

Military alliances at the start of the First World War.

The Arab Revolt

The First World War may have been a purely European issue to begin with, but it soon involved countries from around the world. The Ottoman decision to side with the Germans brought the lands of the Middle East into the conflict.

There was a growing desire among certain Arabs to see more freedom from Ottoman rule. It was felt that there was a lack of Arabic education and not enough regard for Arab culture.

Sharif Hussein bin Ali, leader of the Hashemite Arabs and hereditary ruler of Makkah, wanted to see independent Arab lands covering the Arabian Peninsula and the territories from the Taurus Mountains of southern Turkey to the borders of Iran. The British promised support for his ideals, after agreeing some compromises. In 1916 Hussein launched what was to be known as 'The Arab Revolt'.

▲ The warriors of the Arab Revolt had weapons ranging from swords to rifles. Perhaps their main advantage came from their excellent knowledge of the terrain and their superior riding skills.

British and Arab forces attacked the Hejaz railway, which ran from Damascus to Madinah, as it was an important supply line for the Ottomans. They soon regained control of Makkah and many coastal towns, as well as territory across Palestine and Syria. The First World War ended in 1918 with Germany and the countries that had fought on the same side being defeated.

Hejaz after the war

After the war ended Sharif Hussein declared himself king of an independent state in the Hejaz region of the western Arabian Peninsula.

Activity

Work in a group to discuss possible reasons for Arab involvement in the First World War.

2.12 After the First World War 1

In this lesson you will learn:
- to describe the situation in the Middle Eastern Arab world after the First World War.

Arab hopes dashed

The Ottoman Empire had been the ruling power for hundreds of years but had now lost most of its territories in the region. For many Arabs this presented the opportunity for them to establish independent Arab rule. Hussein had received general support for his ideas from the British representative Sir Henry McMohan.

However, two **diplomats** from France and Britain, François Georges-Picot and Sir Mark Sykes, had also made a secret agreement about what should happen following an Ottoman defeat. The Sykes-Picot agreement divided the formerly Ottoman territories into zones of French and British influence.

The League of Nations

At the end of the First World War a number of governments came together to form The League of Nations. This organisation was created to settle international disputes between nations before they came to the point of war. It was also called upon to decide certain territorial issues following the end of the First World War, including the territories previously under Ottoman control.

League of Nations Mandates

The League of Nations came up with a solution based on the Sykes-Picot agreement, in which the territories would be run by France and Britain as mandates. The mandates were intended to be temporary arrangements which would be in place only until the territories were 'able to stand alone'. No matter how long they were to last, the mandates were seen as a form of continued colonial presence and contradicted the commitments made earlier.

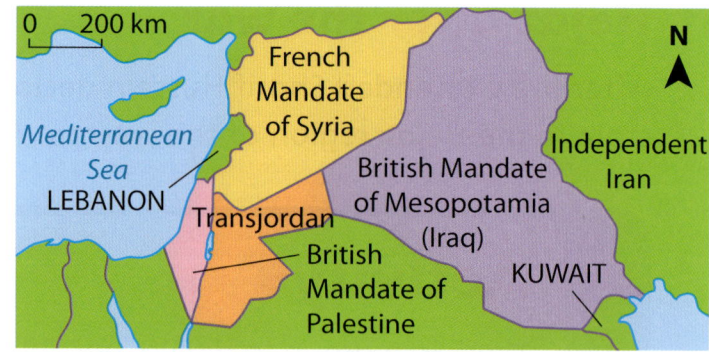

▲ Britain was awarded a mandate over Palestine and Mesopotamia. France was awarded a mandate over Syria and Lebanon.

New nations

The area of the French included Greater Syria which the French divided up to create Lebanon and Syria. Prince Faisal, the third son of Sharif Hussein, declared an independent Syrian government in Damascus in 1918. In 1920 a Pan-Syrian Congress declared an independent Syrian state which covered Syria, Lebanon and Palestine. Prince Faisal became king. After 21 months of this government, the French attitude changed and Faisal was driven out of Syria by the French.

The British mandate territories included Palestine. The principality of Transjordan was created from part of these territories. This was to be ruled over by Abdullah bin al-Hussein, another of Hussein bin Ali's sons. In 1920 there was a popular uprising in the British mandate territories of Mesopotamia, protesting against the continued British presence. In response to this situation it was decided to create the new Kingdom of Iraq. Faisal bin Hussein, who had been driven from Syria by the French, was crowned King Faisal I of Iraq in 1921.

Iraq was granted independence in 1931, although the British maintained a military presence. Faisal bin Hussein ruled until his death in 1933.

▲ King Faisal of Iraq and his brothers in 1923 (front row, left to right: Ali, briefly King of Hejaz; Abdullah, Emir of Jordan; Faisal I of Iraq).

2.13 After the First World War 2

Colonial interests

Following the end of the First World War, the British and the French were clearly making decisions in the region based largely on what would best serve their own interests. At this time both these countries still had significant lands within their empires. These colonies contained resources that were important for use in industries, such as Egyptian cotton for the textile industry. An increasingly important resource found in the countries of the Middle East was oil.

Both Britain and France were also keen to protect shipping and to control trade. The trade routes to India were particularly important for the British.

As we have seen, the Ottoman Empire lost many territories at the end of the First World War. These were divided up by the colonial powers, possibly to try and limit the power and control of trade that such an Arab state could have had.

The Arabian Peninsula

The countries in the Arabian Peninsula included the only Arab lands that had remained largely free of direct European domination. However, these lands were also experiencing a period of change. Powerful tribal and clan leaders still ruled and were trying to create more permanent nations and power bases.

Hussein bin Ali, amongst others, had hoped to see the creation of a single Arab nation from the former Ottoman territories. This idea was denied by the division of former Ottoman territories by the League of Nations, into mandate territories of France and Britain. In the Arabian Peninsula itself, Hussein declared an independent kingdom in the Hejaz. He declared himself king and ruled until 1924.

A rival clan leader, ibn Saud, disputed Hussein's claims to his lands and title. Hussein and his family were driven out of Arabia by the Saudis in 1924. By 1932, ibn Saud overcame his other rivals and declared himself King of Saudi Arabia, which was newly created by joining the Kingdom of Hejaz and the Emirate of the Nejd.

▲ King ibn Saud in 1928.

North Yemen was declared an independent **sovereign state**. In 1926, Imam Yahya, a leader of the Zaydis, declared himself king of the Mutawakkilite Kingdom of Yemen and began to expand his territories and assert his authority.

Although European influence was decreasing, the British were still present in the Trucial States and some other countries of the Arabian Gulf.

During the 1920s the world slowly recovered from the tragedy, slaughter and upheaval of the First World War. At the start of the 1930s there was a financial crisis that created a worldwide economic depression. By the end of the 1930s the world would once again be facing the prospect of war on a global scale.

▲ European industries still needed large amounts of resources from the colonies.

Activity

Make a poster that contains a labelled map showing resources available in different lands of the Middle East, and the main trade routes through the region.

2.14 Independent Arab states

In this lesson you will learn:
- to describe when and how some Arab nations gained their independence.

The Second World War

The Second World War began in September 1939. A man named Adolf Hitler had declared himself ruler of Germany and was determined to bring all of Europe under his control. When he invaded Poland, countries friendly with Poland declared war. Soon countries from all over the world were involved.

The 'Axis powers' included Germany, Italy and Japan. The 'Allies' included Britain, France, Australia, Canada, New Zealand, India, the Soviet Union and the United States. At the end of the war, in 1945, the Axis powers were defeated. Once again, tens of millions had perished, towns and countryside were devastated and economies were ruined.

The aftermath in the wider Arab world

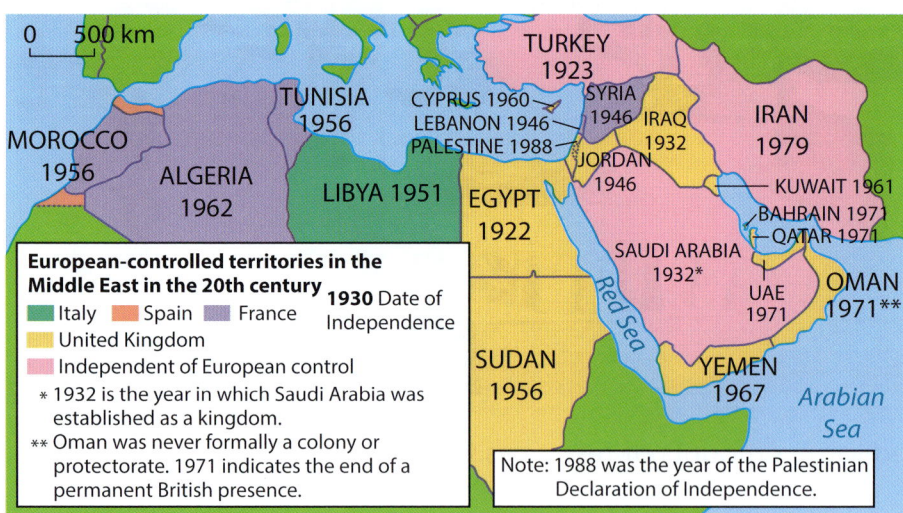

▲ Countries of the Middle East and North Africa gained their independence in the 20th century.

At the end of the Second World War, Britain and France were both re-assessing their ability to maintain their empires and to control trade. In the Middle East, they also faced stronger and more determined efforts for self-rule among the Arab nations. Achieving independence was not a smooth or straightforward process and Arab states gained independence at different times and by different means. This often involved armed conflict and revolution.

Egypt had officially been an independent monarchy since 1922. In 1952 King Farouq, the reigning monarch, was overthrown in a revolution. It was led by two army officers, Muhammad Naguib and Gamal Abdel Nasser. In 1953 Naguib became the first president of the republic of Egypt. He introduced reforms to agricultural practices and began a process of industrialisation. After several years of conflict, British troops were finally forced to withdraw completely in 1956.

◀ Nasser became the second president of Egypt. He carried out many popular actions, including taking control of the Suez Canal in 1956.

Did you know?

In the financial year from April 2013 to April 2014, Egypt received a revenue from the Suez Canal of approximately $5.5 billion in foreign currency.

The Syrian Republic was established in 1930 and a treaty of independence was drawn up in 1936. This was rejected by the French government and the situation was not resolved when the Second World War started. Syria's independence was finally achieved in 1946.

Lebanon gained independence in 1943 but was kept under the control of the allied forces until the end of the Second World War. The last French troops withdrew in 1946.

Iraq had been an independent kingdom since 1932. King Faisal I was followed as king by his son Ghazi. Ghazi died in 1939 and was succeeded by his son, Faisal II, who was only three. Faisal's uncle Abd al-llah acted as regent until he came of age in 1953. A revolution in 1941 saw British troops invade the country in actions that lasted from the 2nd to 31st May. The monarchy was still unpopular, and in another revolution in 1958 King Faisal II was killed and the monarchy abolished.

After some years of instability, the Ba'ath Party eventually came to power in 1968.

Activity

Use the information from this book and other research to make a timeline of Arab independence for countries of the Middle East and North Africa.

2.15 The modern Arabian Gulf

In this lesson you will learn:
- about the formation of the modern countries of the Arabian Peninsula.

Kuwait

Kuwait became a protectorate of Britain in 1899. At the time Kuwait was concerned about Ottoman expansion from the north. The British were concerned about increasing German interests in the area, especially in Iraq.

The boundaries of modern Kuwait were finally established in 1922 and the country became fully independent in June 1961.

▲ Fireworks displays are a common feature of National Day celebrations.

Bahrain

In the last half of the 19th century, Bahrain signed a number of treaties with Britain. Bahrain also participated with the allies in the Second World War. In 1971 Bahrain became a member of the United Nations and the Arab League and signed a new treaty of friendship with the United Kingdom.

Qatar

The Qataris removed the Ottomans from Doha in 1915 and many took part in the Arab revolt against them between 1916 and 1918. Qatar became a British protectorate in 1916, partly to avoid becoming part of Saudi Arabia. Pressure for British removal grew in strength in the 1950s and 1960s and Qatar gained independence in 1971.

The United Arab Emirates

Towards the end of the 20th century, the seven 'Trucial Sheikdoms', together with Bahrain and Qatar, considered forming a union of emirates. Qatar and Bahrain opted to become independent states. The Trucial Sheikdoms became independent in 1971. Abu Dhabi and Dubai emirates decided to form a union and invited the other emirates to join. The emirates of Sharjah, Ajman, Umm Al Qaiwain and Fujairah did so on the 2nd December 1971. Ras al-Khaimah joined in early 1972 to complete what is today's United Arab Emirates.

▲ Flags and national costumes are another feature of independence celebrations.

Oman

British relationships with Oman had first been established by the British East India Trading Company in the 17th century. The British government signed treaties in 1798 and 1800 that created closer relationships with Oman as the French increased their power in the region. Further treaties of 'peace, friendship and navigation' were signed in 1891, 1939 and 1951. Oman was never a formal colony or protectorate of Britain, and the withdrawal of British influence happened more slowly than in the rest of the Gulf region.

Saudi Arabia

The formation of the modern kingdom of Saudi Arabia is generally understood to have begun in 1902 when Abdulaziz bin Saud took the city garrison in Riyadh from the rival al-Rashid family. Abdulaziz conquered the rest of the Hejaz and brought many tribes together. By 1925 he controlled Makkah and Madinah. The country was named the Kingdom of Saudi Arabia in 1932.

Activity

Add information from this text and other research to the 'Timeline of Arab independence' begun in the previous lesson.

2.16 Rapid development

In this lesson you will learn:
- to describe features of the development of modern countries of the Arabian Peninsula.

Development

Development is a process of change and growth. As a country develops, its economy changes and grows stronger. The **standard of living** and sense of wellbeing of the population should improve.

Part of development involves creating opportunities for employment, either in government departments or in private companies. Development also involves providing a good education system that allows people to gain the knowledge and skills they need. Development is also about an improvement in health and the experience of a secure and happy life. Part of this comes from providing a good health service.

All these challenges faced the countries of the Arabian Gulf when they became independent. Although the process often takes a very long time, the money from oil revenues has allowed these countries to transform themselves very rapidly.

▲ By 1990 the development of Dubai was well underway.

> **Did you know?**
> The countries of the Arabian Gulf have the first and third tallest buildings in the world: the Burj Khalifa in Dubai and the Makkah Royal Clock Tower Hotel in Makkah.

Oil and gas revenue

Oil had been discovered in the region in the 1930s. Some development of the industry had taken place although this was usually under the control of multi-national oil companies.

On becoming independent, the oil producing states often took greater control over the revenues, either by **nationalising** the industry or taking greater shares in the private operating companies. The oil-producing countries also had to negotiate new relationships with the industrialised nations of the west who were the main customers for the oil.

The effects of development

At independence, local populations were small and lacked skills and expertise in many areas. While the national education systems were being developed, many people travelled overseas to receive education and training in specialised fields. At the same time, people from other countries who already had the necessary skills and qualifications moved into the region. The massive amount of construction that needed to be carried out also drew in huge numbers of workers. A major effect of rapid development has therefore been the rapid and dramatic increase in the population and the creation of a multicultural society.

The constant efforts to improve education facilities have meant that literacy levels are now very high. Increasing numbers of people have been able to gain the skills and training they need within the region.

The countries of the Arabian Gulf have been transformed from areas with few roads and basic amenities into places where people can enjoy a high standard of living in cities with world class facilities and services.

▲ The Arabian Gulf has some of the world's most modern cities. This is Dubai today.

Activity

Write an article for a travel guide that gives a brief history of the development of your country since independence.

Unit 2 Review questions

1. When several members of a single family rule in succession, this is called:
   a. an aristocracy
   b. a monarchy
   c. a dynasty
   d. a senate

2. When one country is politically controlled by another distant country it is called:
   a. a municipality
   b. a colony
   c. a region
   d. an island

3. In the 1500s, the Portuguese wanted to take the town of Hormuz as this would help them control trade in:
   a. the Red Sea
   b. the Indian Ocean
   c. the Arabian Gulf
   d. the Suez Canal

4. At the beginning of the 19th century, the French tried to colonise Egypt. They were defeated by:
   a. the Ottoman Empire and the Germans
   b. the Ottoman Empire and the British
   c. the Ottoman Empire and the Dutch
   d. the Ottoman Empire and the Austrians

5. The countries of the Middle East and Arabian Peninsula were all independent by:
   a. the end of the 20th century
   b. the end of the Second World War
   c. the end of the 19th century
   d. the beginning of the Second Word War

6. Referring to the table below, write the letters for the events listed below in the chronological order that matches the dates shown in the 'Year' column.

Event	Year
a Outbreak of First World War	1515
b Nasser takes control of Suez Canal	1801
c Albuquerque takes Hormuz	1914
d French defeated in Egypt	1956

7. What was a major effect of the opening of the Suez Canal in 1869?
   a. The population of Cairo increased
   b. Goods could be transported to the Mediterranean Sea without being carried over land
   c. The price of fish decreased
   d. Ibn Saud became King of Saudi Arabia

8. Describe some of the reasons why European nations began colonising other countries in the 19th century.

9. Describe some ways in which the countries of the Arabian Gulf have changed regarding population size, multiculturalism, education and industry since they gained independence.

3 People and places

In this unit you will learn:
- how to use maps to identify world regions
- about worldwide population distributions and urbanisation
- about climate change, and strategies to deal with it
- how to create a sustainable world
- how to understand our modern world – trade, transport and tourism
- to prepare reports, articles, speeches and presentations.

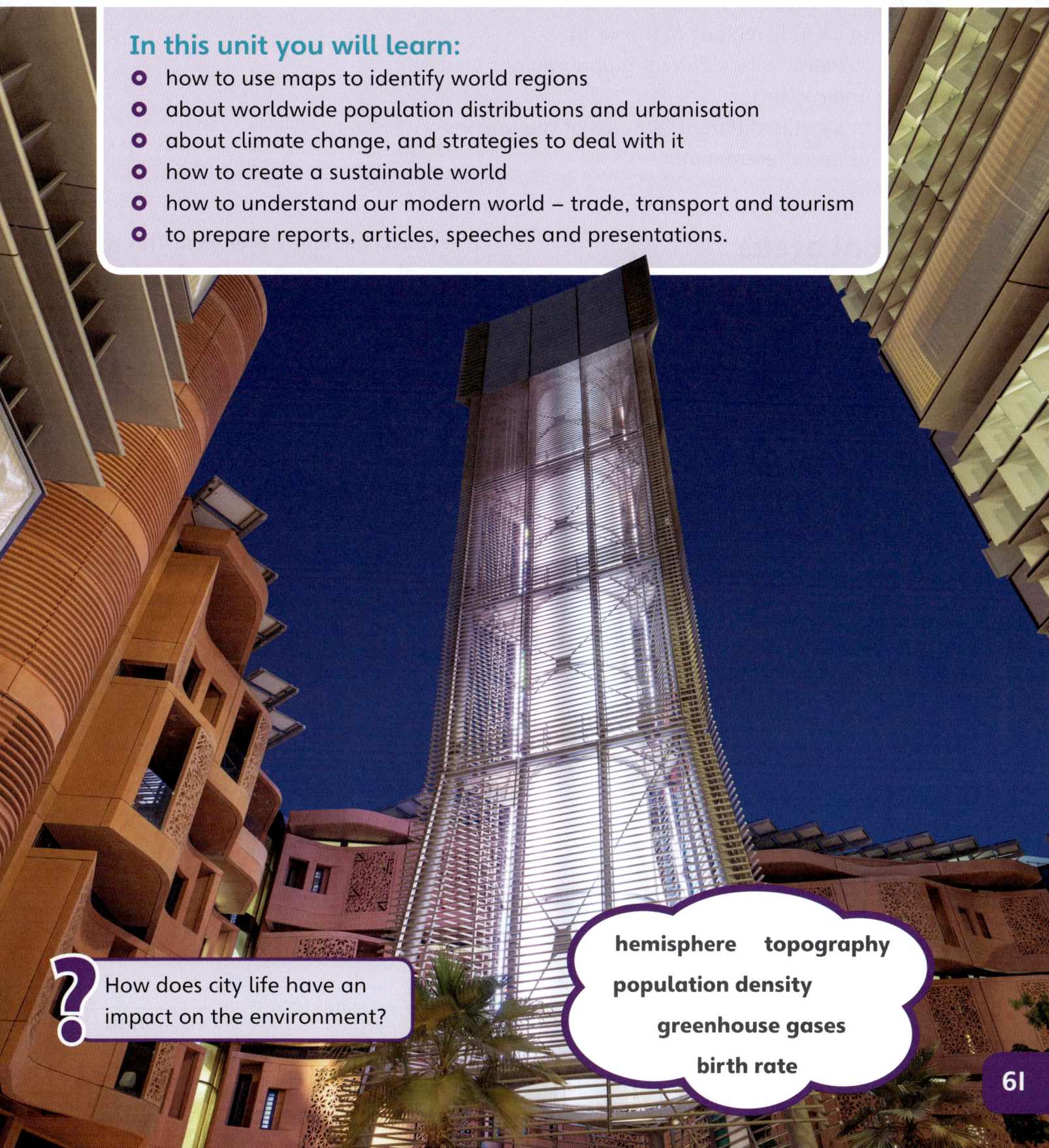

? How does city life have an impact on the environment?

hemisphere   topography
population density
greenhouse gases
birth rate

3.1 Using maps and globes

In this lesson you will learn:
- to identify regions of the world
- to identify the different global regions on maps and globes
- to identify different features of the regions using different maps.

Global areas

We use specific terms to describe locations in geography. The major division of the Earth is into **hemispheres**.

For descriptive purposes, the Earth is divided into a northern hemisphere and a southern hemisphere by the imaginary line of the equator.

The Earth is divided into western and eastern hemispheres by an imaginary line called the Prime Meridian. This is a line of longitude that runs through Greenwich in England.

The world's regions, as we describe them, help us to identify areas that have similar characteristics. These similarities are in both the physical and human geography of the region. These two aspects are connected because the physical geography of an area often affects the human geography.

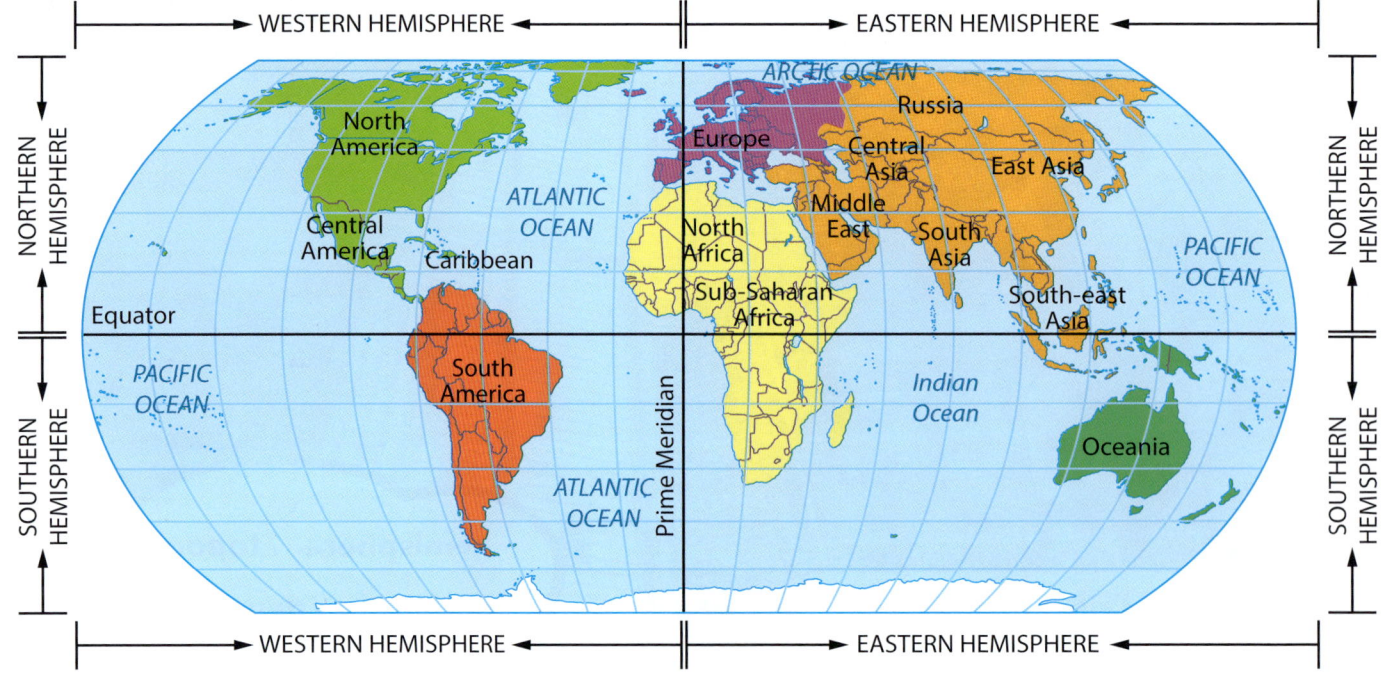

▲ The regions of the world.

People have always moved across the face of the planet looking for suitable places in which to live. The suitability of the area for human habitation has been determined by many factors including the availability of resources, the climate and the **terrain**. These factors are often similar across all the lands in the areas we describe as regions. Factors like climate and terrain also result in other similarities, for example the types of natural vegetation or how suitable the area is for agriculture.

There can also be a number of cultural characteristics across a region, based around the foods available and the types of clothing worn as a result of the climate. Similar ideas and principles can also guide the behaviour and values of people within a region. Although the languages and cultures of individual countries within a region can be different, it is possible to identify a regional culture. For example we can recognise a Middle Eastern culture and tell it apart from an African or South-east-Asian or European culture.

The countries within a geographical region also often face similar challenges, again as a result of geographical features. These challenges can be a result of the climate or dominant weather systems and can take the form of regular tropical storms or long periods of drought.

The similarities in geographical and geological conditions can also mean that countries within a region have similar natural resources and are therefore able to produce similar goods. This can present challenges when these countries consider trading with one another and with countries in other parts of the world.

▲ Regions of the world often develop distinctive characteristics.

Activity

Use physical, climate, vegetation and population maps to explore a region of the Earth. Make a presentation that explains why people have inhabited this area, and what the similarities and differences are between the physical and human geography across the region.

3.2 Population distribution

In this lesson you will learn:
- to explain factors that create patterns of population distribution and density
- to describe and discuss urbanisation
- to describe and discuss migration.

Population distribution and density

Throughout history, human populations have spread across the surface of the planet, to live wherever they could adapt to the local conditions and wherever their basic needs for water, food and shelter could be met. In the past these patterns were mostly caused by different conditions of climate, **topography** and vegetation. These varied and so the distribution of populations was not even and the **population density** also varied.

When people move from one area to another, this is called migration. Past migrations of people have occurred for various reasons. In some cases, the climate altered so that people were either confined within a particular area or, if favourable conditions were found in wider areas, were able to spread out into new areas. Migration was also often driven by the ability of a given area to support a population. If the population grew too large, then some people would leave and seek out a new place to settle.

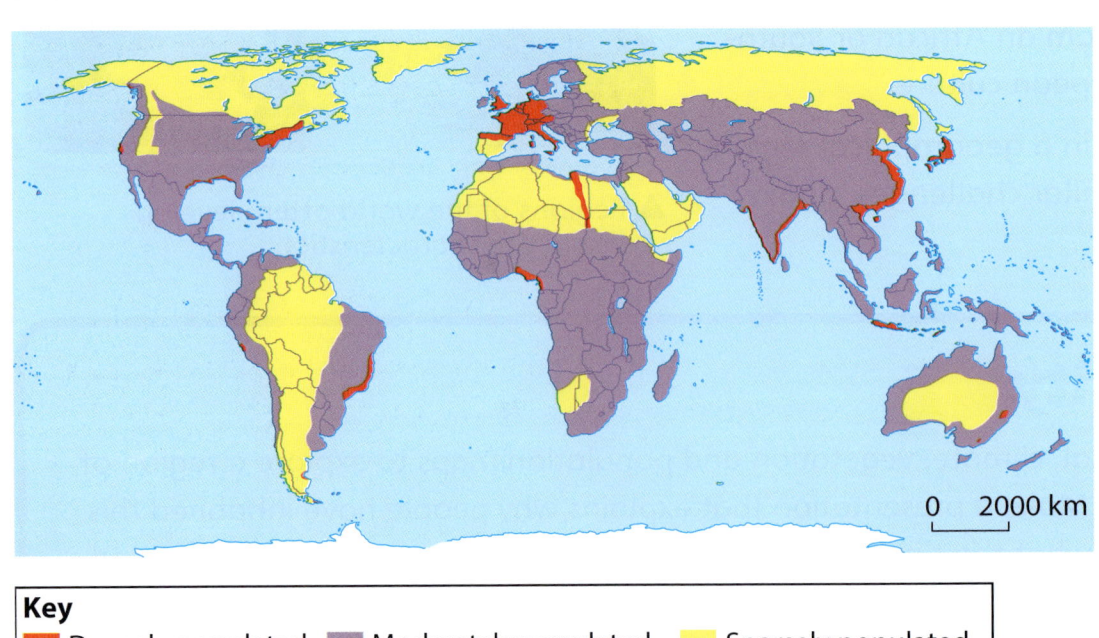

Key
- Densely populated
- Moderately populated
- Sparsely populated

▲ Maps of global population density are easy to read but they do not make clear where populations in certain areas are especially high.

> **Did you know?**
>
> The most densely populated country in the Arabian Gulf is Bahrain, with 1,646 people per square kilometre. The most densely populated area in the world is the Macau region of China, with 18,534 people per square kilometre.

Factors such as economic development, the exploration and exploitation of resources have added to the 'survival factors' that influenced early settlement patterns.

As human societies have developed there has been an increasing use of the Earth's resources and an increasing range of human activity. The need to live close to resources such as food and water has slowly decreased as methods of production and transportation have changed. The location of human populations is now as much to do with economic activity and work opportunities as with being near essential resources. This is partly why so many people now live in cities.

The effects of migration

People in one area may feel that there are limited opportunities for employment where they currently live. These people may therefore migrate to another area or country in search of work. The area from which such people come may have fewer facilities and amenities, such as energy and water supplies, shops and healthcare. As more people leave, the level of provision of these facilities and amenities will drop even further, prompting more people to leave.

▲ What facilities might suffer in a small community like this if too many people move away?

Meanwhile, in the places to which these people move, the systems for education and health, water and energy supplies experience greater pressure.

Activity

Write a brief report that explains the factors that influence the pattern of human population distribution and density. Give examples of how this pattern is reflected in three different parts of the world.

3.3 World population

In this lesson you will learn:
- to identify features of the world population
- to understand the possible consequences of continued world population growth
- to suggest ways of dealing with issues in the future.

Issues connected with population

The population of the world currently exceeds 7 billion. 78 million more people are added to the global population every year. The United Nations predicts that by 2050 the world's population will reach 9 billion. Almost all the growth is taking place in less economically developed countries (LEDCs). Approximately 97 out of every 100 births are in these countries. Many of these countries already struggle to provide the basic needs of the existing population.

Nations across the globe face different situations. People are living longer in more economically developed countries (MEDCs), due to improvements in healthcare. These countries have to consider what happens when more of the population is elderly. LEDCs have fast-growing populations which puts pressure on services such as education and health and on water supply and waste disposal systems.

▲ What special requirements and needs do older people have?

Population growth and poverty

Germany is a rich developed country with a population of approximately 83 million. Ethiopia is a less developed country also with a population of 83 million. Germany has a low **birth rate** and the population is predicted to fall to 75 million by 2050. Ethiopia's birth rate is 4.6 and its population could almost double to 145 million over the same period.

In 2011, 70 percent of the people in Ethiopia lived on less than US$2 a day. If issues around poverty are not addressed what will happen in countries like Ethiopia?

Benefits of education and smaller families

A key factor in addressing population growth and reducing poverty is the education of women and girls. Poverty brings a lack of choices because of a lack of money. Research shows that when women and girls in less developed countries receive education then the birth rate drops. Without so many children to feed, it becomes more likely that a family will be able to rise out of poverty.

If parents choose to have fewer children, then a family is more able to meet its needs. If there is more time between births, the health of mother and child is better. Women have more options to work, earn money and increase the income of the family. All this benefits the community too.

▲ When health services improve and parents think more children will survive, then women have fewer children.

If a country has a fixed amount to spend on education and health, then a smaller population will mean that resources are shared between fewer people so the quality of these services improves. Investing in the future human resources of the country means that the long-term prospects for the country improve.

Activities

1. Carry out some research to find out where in the world people are undernourished or go hungry through lack of food.
2. Work in a group to suggest some ideas that would mean that everyone in the world had enough to eat.

3.4 Urbanisation

In this lesson you will learn:
- to describe the process of urbanisation
- to identify factors that lead to urbanisation
- to describe some consequences of urbanisation.

Urbanisation

For most of human history the majority of people have worked in agriculture and so have lived in rural areas. The minority of people who lived in the urban areas of towns and cities relied on the much greater numbers of agricultural workers to provide the food.

The 18th and 19th centuries saw a great change in agriculture in a number of countries that were becoming industrialised. Changes in agricultural practices meant fewer people were needed to keep the supply of food available. With no work in the local rural area, people moved elsewhere, often to a town or city. Here they hoped to find employment, possibly in one of the new factories that were also being built in this period.

As more countries around the world have become industrialised, so an increasing proportion of the world's population is living in cities. This process of increased urban living is called urbanisation.

◀ The world has recently passed the point where, for the first time in history, more people are living in towns and cities than in the countryside.

Around the world people feel attracted to the benefits of the urban areas. These include a greater range of services like health and education, better facilities, including water, **sanitation** and electricity supplies, and more amenities such as parks and entertainment venues.

Many people also feel pushed from the rural areas because there is little work and few prospects for improvement.

Problems of urbanisation

Urbanisation does create some problems. Most people do not live very near their place of work and so they have to travel. Traffic congestion means that the roads become blocked. The emissions from all the vehicles can affect the quality of the air.

Although the services in an urban area may be better than those in rural areas, they are put under greater pressure as more people move into that area. Increasing numbers of people have to be supplied with drinking water, for example. Greater numbers of people means that more waste has to be dealt with.

When more people want to live in a particular area it makes the price of land and housing increase. Sometimes this means that only a certain group of people can afford to live there.

When people leave their rural communities there is an even smaller population left to work in local agriculture and to support local businesses. These businesses may have to close and other services may be cut.

◀ In some countries people move to the city but cannot afford proper housing. They build 'shanty towns' which do not have proper water supplies or sanitation.

Activity

Write an article for a magazine that describes the process of urbanisation and explains some of its causes and effects.

3.5 Climate change

In this lesson you will learn:
- about climate change
- to suggest strategies to reduce the problem.

Climate change

There are complicated natural systems that control the Earth's climate. When some parts of the system alter this can cause changes in the climate. This has happened naturally many times in the past.

Temperature is an important part of the Earth's climate. The Earth is heated by rays from the sun that pass through the layers of gases that make up the atmosphere. In normal conditions many of these rays hit the Earth's surface and are then reflected back. Some reflected rays travel back through the atmosphere and into space and others are reflected back again by **greenhouse gases**.

▲ In a greenhouse the sun's rays pass through the glass or other material of the greenhouse and warm up everything inside it. A lot of the heat energy is trapped inside.

Certain amounts of greenhouse gases are needed to trap some heat and keep the Earth at the right temperature. Many scientists argue that people are creating a problem because they are burning too many fossil fuels. This creates more greenhouse gases, such as carbon dioxide, and is causing a problem because more heat is being trapped and so the average temperature on the Earth's surface is increasing. These scientists say that this rise in temperature is likely to result in a number of environmental problems.

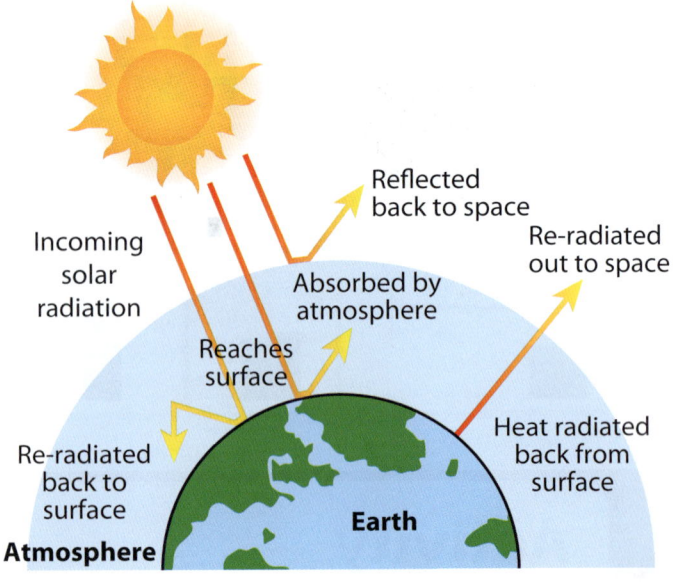

▲ Global warming and the greenhouse effect.

Road transport, electricity production and heating and cooling homes and workplaces are the main causes of greenhouse emissions.

Global problems associated with climate change

The predictions associated with climate change, and especially with increasing temperatures include:

- Rising sea levels: low-lying coastal areas may experience much more frequent flooding or even be lost beneath the sea completely. Coastal areas are often important as flood defences and they also act as **habitats** for species of wildlife.
- Inland flooding: this is expected more frequently in many countries with permanent river systems.
- Higher temperatures: these could lead to an increase in ill-health and even death. High temperatures often result in poorer air quality and in increased pollution so there may be more instances of conditions such as asthma.
- Unpredictable and extreme weather: this would have serious impacts on agriculture in different parts of the world where prolonged droughts make sowing and growing crops much harder or where heavy rains ruin crops or wash away soil.
- Loss of habitat: the existing pattern of habitats could change, with some colder types of habitat retreating towards the polar regions with all the animal and plant species being squeezed into a smaller area and ultimately decreasing in number.

▲ Some scientists predict loss of animal habitats due to climate change.

Activity

Hold a class discussion on why climate change is an important issue and how it should be addressed.

3.6 Sustainability

In this lesson you will learn:
- about sustainability
- to describe sustainable development
- to describe sustainable use of resources.

Sustainability

Sustainability means using the resources of the planet so that people today can meet their needs without making it difficult for people in the future to do the same. The issue of sustainability challenges people to think about the impact that their activities have on other people, on the environment and on the economy, both locally and globally. It makes people think about the way resources are used now and how human activities in the future can be carried out in ways that make the best possible use of resources.

▲ New technologies that make use of renewable resources can help achieve sustainable development.

Footprints

The word 'footprints' has been adopted to talk about some of the impacts that people have on the Earth.

A 'carbon footprint' is to do with the amount of carbon dioxide (and other greenhouse gases) produced when an activity is carried out or when something, such as a car, is made.

A 'water footprint' is to do with the amount of water used to make a product, including the water used in irrigating crops.

An 'eco footprint' is taken to mean all the land used to produce energy, to create all the things we use and to deal with all the waste we generate. The richer, more developed countries use a larger proportion per person than the less developed countries.

Sustainable development

The countries of the world are sometimes put into groups according to their stage of development. 'Human development' is about the amount of access people have to money, jobs, health, education, nutrition, leisure, safety and security. 'Economic development' is to do with a country's wealth and where this comes from. For example, an economy based on simple, small-scale agriculture is considered to be less developed than an economy based around industry or financial services.

In most cases human and economic development are closely linked. The economy of a country needs to be strong and growing if the population is to see an improvement in the quality of life.

The 'developed' countries in the world today achieved their development in the past by using large amounts of resources. There are not enough resources on the planet for the development of all countries to be achieved in the same way. The challenge for the future is to find a way for countries to develop but without using resources in an unsustainable way.

▲ Education is an essential part of human development.

Activity

Prepare a lesson you would deliver to younger students that explains the idea of sustainable development simply. Include examples of how they could consume fewer resources.

3.7 Sustainable cities

In this lesson you will learn:
- how cities need to be adapted to suit future needs.

Sustainable cities

More people are living in cities than ever before and the trend is expected to continue. Population densities in cities are high and so cities use more resources, produce more waste and generate more global greenhouse gas emissions than rural areas.

> **Did you know?**
> Greenhouse gases including carbon dioxide are produced in manufacturing solar panels. Even so, generating electricity from these is said to produce 20 times less carbon dioxide than generating electricity by burning coal and 10 times less than burning gas.

The way cities are designed, built and used has to meet the requirements of today's citizens but also respond to the environmental situation.

In recent years people have seen the need for cities to be developed in a more sustainable way. There are a number of features a city needs if it is to be sustainable:

- Safe and reliable public transport that is seen as a realistic alternative to the private car
- Safe environments to walk or cycle
- Accessible public areas that feel safe and enjoyable
- Good use of renewable resources
- Reduction in use of non-renewable resources to a minimum level
- Recycling systems for different materials in place
- Waste reduced to a minimum
- Water used wisely
- A population containing a mixture of people from different backgrounds
- Strong communities containing active citizens
- Social and cultural facilities that everyone can access
- A sustainable rate of growth.

It is sometimes harder to achieve sustainability in existing areas where older building techniques and materials have been used. For example, some buildings were designed and built in a way that make it difficult to control the temperature, whether heating or cooling. This is important in places with an extreme climate. In places with high temperatures like the Arabian Gulf, a lot of energy is used to keep buildings cool by running air-conditioning units.

The physical infrastructure such as the existing road network cannot always cope with increases in traffic that arise from a rapidly growing population. It is not always possible to create efficient transport networks or to build new public transport systems.

◀ The centuries-old idea of using wind towers to provide natural cooling is used in Masdar City, a new development in Abu Dhabi that aims to have the smallest possible environmental impact.

It is easier to ensure that all new development takes issues of sustainability into account. Modern cities can be built using the smallest amount possible of non-renewable resources. The design can also ensure that the best use can be made of renewable resources, for example using solar power to provide electrical energy or heating for water.

Countries of the Arabian Gulf are fortunate because they are very modern and have been able to incorporate these ideas into the layout of whole cities and into the designs of individual buildings. Using tall buildings to create shade and structures to capture cooling winds helps reduce energy from fossil fuels. Solar and wind energy can also be exploited to provide electricity.

◀ People move around Masdar City in electric transit vehicles, electric cars and hybrid low emission buses.

Activity

Work in a group to design a sustainable city.

3.8 Deforestation

In this lesson you will learn:
- about the global problem of deforestation
- to suggest strategies to reduce the problem.

Deforestation

Deforestation means the removal of trees. This is happening at a very rapid rate in many different places on the planet. The Food and Agriculture Organisation of the United Nations estimates that 13 million hectares of forest were lost through natural causes or changed to another use each year in the first decade of the 21st century. This is approximately the same as losing an area the size of 36 football pitches every minute.

Causes of deforestation

Many forests are cleared because commercial logging companies cut down all the trees in an area, even though only some of them have commercial value. Many of the most valuable trees are in rainforests and other sensitive environments, such as areas of higher altitude bamboo forests. The forests are often found in poorer, less developed countries.

▲ Huge areas of rainforest and other woodlands are destroyed every day.

In some countries forests are cleared to grow a cash crop, such as palm oil, or to provide grazing or food for livestock. The soil quickly becomes less fertile. Expensive fertilisers have to be used and many farmers cannot afford them. Those who can do not always use them safely and they can be a threat to people's health.

Forests are also cleared for mining or quarrying. The trees are removed and much of the landscape is damaged. In these cases the soil will never recover and the area becomes quite useless. Logging and extractive industries clear trees to build roads to move equipment and products. The roads allow others to move into the forest areas where they clear areas for farming or houses.

Forests are often cleared to make way for the new or expanding settlements that are needed to house the growing global population.

Many people in the developing world still rely on wood as their main source of fuel for heating and cooking. As these populations grow, more trees are cut down.

Problems with deforestation

Deforestation gives rise to the following problems:

- loss of habitats for plants and animals
- decline in the numbers of species of animals and plants
- loss of sources of important products, including the basic ingredients of some medicines
- soil erosion
- flooding
- global warming through areas that have been cleared by burning
- loss of the beneficial effect of trees taking in carbon dioxide
- loss of moisture retention in trees and imbalance of the climate.

▲ Deforestation destroys the habitat of many kinds of animal.

Activities

1 Work in a group to:
   - find out about deforestation in one country in the world
   - find out about the use of timber and wood products in your country and how people can find wood from sustainable sources
   - suggest ways in which the word's forests might be protected.
2 Prepare a speech for a public meeting which is opposing a new quarry that will remove some forest. Your speech should explain the importance of the forest and the problems associated with deforestation.

3.9 Trade

In this lesson you will learn:
- to identify and describe domestic and international trade
- to identify the trade links with countries around the world.

Trade

Trade is the exchange of goods and services. Trade takes place because individuals, companies and countries have different needs. The amount of goods and services customers want to buy is called the demand. The amount of goods and services that businesses produce is called the supply.

Domestic trade

Domestic trade is the exchange of goods within a country. The consumers in a country make up the 'domestic market'. In early history most trade was in the domestic market because transport did not provide access to an international market. Truly domestic trade is limited by the resources available and the products that can be made. The advantage of domestic trade is that it keeps money within a country where it can help local economies to grow. This is partly why people are being encouraged to buy food that is produced locally.

Most countries today have a mixture of domestic and international trade.

International trade

Countries trade with one another because they have different resources available. Goods and services bought by one country from another are called imports. The goods and services sold by one country to another country are called exports. Countries earn money from exports but have to spend money on imports. Countries want to make more money from exports than they spend on imports.

▲ Goods are imported and exported through ports along the Arabian Gulf.

As countries develop, the types of things they import and export can change. In more developed countries the main exports are expensive manufactured goods such as machinery, cars, medicines and electronics. Less developed countries often export primary products that have lower value, such as tea and other foods. Developed countries also export services such as banking and consultancy.

Countries also specialise. This means they focus on using the resources they have to the greatest effect. For example, Ghana in West Africa is one of the largest producers of cocoa in the world. In countries where there is a good deal of land, such as Canada, other agricultural goods such as cereal crops are more important. In countries where labour costs are cheaper, such as China, manufacturing becomes important. As countries specialise they are less able to meet all their own needs. Goods and services need to be exchanged and all countries become more interdependent. An importing country relies on the goods and services from elsewhere to meet some of its needs. An exporting country needs the importing country to act as a market for its goods and services.

Trade agreements

Today many countries have special trade agreements which establish the terms for trade between them. The World Trade Organisation is the body that deals with the rules of international trade and aims to make this trade easy and fair.

Trading blocs

In some cases countries within a region form a special trading union. The Co-operation Council for the Arab States of the Gulf (GCC) works towards the integration of a number of countries in the Arabian Gulf region in matters including trade. All member countries adopt policies that make trading between them easier. They can also act as a united body in matters of international trade.

▲ Countries have different and unique climates, landscapes and cultural heritage. They can therefore offer a tourism service to people who wish to visit a landscape such as the one shown here.

Activity

Work in a group to identify and describe imports and exports in your country. Explain what your findings show, especially in respect of food security.

3.10 Transport connections

In this lesson you will learn:
- to identify the transportation links with countries around the world.

As the world has become increasingly complex the distances that people and goods travel have increased. Transportation has become ever more sophisticated.

Air transport

Air transportation provides one of the most important links between different places in the world.

Many people today choose to fly to another country for holidays where they can experience different cultures and climates. Business people also fly around the world for meetings and negotiations.

The speed with which distances can be covered using air travel means that it is very useful for trade and business. Some goods need to be used while they are still fresh, such as foods and flowers. These can now be transported to markets thousands of miles away from the producers. Items that need to be received quickly can be couriered by air.

> **Did you know?**
> The international airports of the countries of the Arabian Gulf handled over 184 million passengers in 2013.

▲ According to figures from the Airports Council International, the total number of passengers using Dubai airport in 2013 was 66,431,533. This placed it as the seventh busiest airport in the world. It was also the fifth busiest cargo hub, with 2,435,567 metric tonnes of cargo being handled.

Sea transport

Shipping routes across the seas and oceans of the world are still an important part of global transportation.

Huge ships carry vast amounts of goods around the world every day. The amount that a single ship can carry on one journey makes it an efficient and economic means of transport.

Ports on the Arabian Gulf are cargo hubs and deal with importing and exporting goods. They are also important places for re-exporting goods. This happens when goods are unloaded from one ship and reloaded onto one or more other ships to travel to other countries.

Passenger transport by sea is mostly on cruise ships. Shorter distances are covered by ferries and these are often used for more regular journeys.

▲ Deep-water harbours can accommodate large cargo ships and cruise liners.

Land transport

International transportation of cargo over land makes use of large trucks by roads and freight trains by rail. Long-distance international passenger journeys also take place by bus, coach or train.

Transportation and the environment

All modes of modern transportation have an environmental impact. Creating the physical infrastructure involves taking land that could be used for other purposes and uses large amounts of resources such as concrete, stone and steel. The transportation itself, largely reliant on burning fossil fuels, produces emissions which adversely affect local air quality and the atmosphere.

The challenge for the future is to balance the need for the global movement of goods while minimising the environmental harm.

Activity

Write about the advantages and disadvantages, including the environmental impact, of three different types of transport used to move goods and people throughout the world.

3.11 Tourism

In this lesson you will learn:
- to define tourism
- to identify economic and social issues connected with tourism
- to identify attractions that appeal to tourists including some physical features of the Arab world.

Tourism and its impact

Tourism is the business of providing services for tourists, including organising their travel, hotels and entertainment. Most tourism is for recreation or leisure but it can also have a more particular focus, for example religious or business tourism.

Tourism has a positive effect on a country's economy because it brings in foreign money but there are several issues to consider:

- Land that could be used for purposes such as agriculture is given over to hotels and other facilities.
- Tourists arriving in large numbers effectively cause an increase in the population. More resources, including food, are needed to meet their needs.
- Tourists also put extra pressure on such things as water supplies and waste disposal systems.
- There may be social issues with people from different cultures. For example, tourists may need to be asked to show respect for a sacred place and to dress appropriately.

▲ Land has to be given over to provide tourist accommodation and the coasts are a popular location.

The Arabian Gulf as a tourist destination

The Arabian Gulf is becoming increasingly established as a popular tourist destination. Many countries in this area have been able to develop a tourism industry because they are able to offer some of the things that tourists from other parts of the world want. For example, the hot, dry climate appeals to travellers from cooler, wetter places.

Arabian Gulf countries also have natural features which are very different from those found in the countries of Europe or in North America. These include:

- the desert landscapes
- mountainous regions with features such as caves
- unique sights such as the 'inland sea' of Khor Al Adaiad in Qatar
- oases and coastal wetlands
- exceptional coral reefs.

These places and environments need to be cared for and protected as they are parts of the natural world. The fact that they can act as tourist attractions and so generate an economic benefit is an added incentive for this. Popularity with tourists can also be the biggest threat to preserving their beauty and so the industry has to be carefully managed and properly regulated.

▲ Wildlife and marine reserves can be places that bring benefit to both wildlife and tourists.

Tourists often want to experience something of the culture and heritage of the places they visit. There are many opportunities for cultural tourism within the countries of the Arabian Gulf. People can experience contemporary and traditional Arab culture as well as finding out more of the history of these lands and peoples.

Activity

Write an article for a European newspaper that describes a tourist's visit to your country. You should recommend that other people try this experience for themselves.

Unit 3 Review questions

1. The number of people living in a given area is described as the:
   a population distribution
   b working population
   c rural population
   d population density

2. The process that sees more people living in towns and cities rather than in the countryside is called:
   a urban sprawl
   b urbanisation
   c immigration
   d evacuation

3. Sustainability is best described as:
   a using the planet's resources in a way that meets the needs of people today and allows for people in the future to meet their needs
   b sharing the planet's resources equally between people everywhere
   c using only renewable resources
   d using the planet's resources to create re-usable items that will not need to be replaced

4. Pressure is exerted on education and health services, water supplies and waste disposal by:
   a a decreasing population
   b an ageing population
   c a rapidly growing population
   d a mobile population

5. The countries of the regions of the Middle East and North Africa are all in the northern hemisphere.
   a True
   b False

6. The countries of the regions of the Middle East and North Africa are all in the western hemisphere.
   a True
   b False

7. Cargo ships are an efficient means of transporting goods because they:
   a move slowly
   b can reach harbours in many countries around the world
   c can travel across the widest oceans
   d can carry large amounts of goods on a single journey

8. Write a brief report that explains what domestic trade is and why it should be encouraged.

9. Describe some of the features of the Arabian Gulf that might attract tourists and some of the issues that could arise from tourism in these places.

10. Write about five features you would expect to see in a sustainable city.

11. Describe some of the issues you feel are important concerning climate change.

4 Citizenship

In this unit you will learn:
- about globalisation and its effects
- about global inequality
- how we can use resources carefully and reduce waste
- about new means of communication
- how all citizens can be involved in society
- to create a simple flow chart
- to use the internet effectively.

? In what ways do you feel that you are a 'global citizen'?

water cycle   sedimentary   hyperlink
tectonic plate   search engine   web browser
biodiversity   policies   vote   election   federal
direct democracy   representative democracy
profitability   financial services

4.1 Globalisation

In this lesson you will learn:
- about globalisation
- to identify the effects of globalisation on different aspects of life.

Globalisation

Globalisation is the name given to the process in which individuals, groups, businesses and countries around the world become increasingly interdependent. It is in many ways a process that has been happening slowly over a long period of time. Recent advances in technology have speeded up the process dramatically and global interconnections are more obvious than ever.

Globalisation and trade

Countries and businesses are linked around the world by trade. To enjoy the benefits of trade these countries and businesses are therefore dependent on one another.

This interdependence is made clearer today through improved communications. Although globalisation has brought a huge range of goods to consumers it has also made them more aware of the environmental and social impact of obtaining resources and goods manufactured in distant places.

Globalisation and work

One effect of globalisation is that many people move away from their place of birth to live and work in another country. Some people from poorer countries send money home to support relatives.

Globalisation also affects the kind of work available in different places. Many companies today are 'multi-national' which means that they operate in different countries.

▲ The global textile and clothing industry employs millions of people.

Manufacturing now takes place much more in places like China and South-east Asia than in industrialised countries in Europe. This is partly because the labour is much cheaper in these places. It is important, however, that people here have good working conditions and receive fair wages.

Globalisation and information

Technology, especially use of the internet, has changed the way people all over the world communicate, learn and carry out business. These technological advances have made a huge difference to the success of many ventures and have given people access to new ways of learning and achieving self-improvement. Technology is not available to everyone and those without access to it are disadvantaged.

Globalisation and culture

For some people globalisation means the introduction of a uniform global culture all around the world. They fear that this will override the traditional cultures of individual countries and regions and the values, ideas and beliefs on which these are based.

No matter how people feel about globalisation, there is no escaping the fact that we are all global citizens.

▲ Global brands provide similar experiences around the world.

Activity

Describe the effect that globalisation has had on society and employment opportunities in your country.

4.2 Global issues 1

In this lesson you will learn:
- about the reasons for uneven global resource distribution.

Inequality of resource distribution

People use natural resources to meet their needs for food, fuel and shelter. The amount of resources available in any one location determines the size of population that place can support.

The distribution of resources refers to the way these are spread out around the world. Resources are not distributed equally around the world.

Basic resources include water, land, vegetation, animals, minerals and fossil fuels.

Water

The amount of water available in any one area depends on a range of natural conditions and natural processes, including the **water cycle**. The overall climate is particularly significant and so are local natural features such as high ground or the presence of bodies of water.

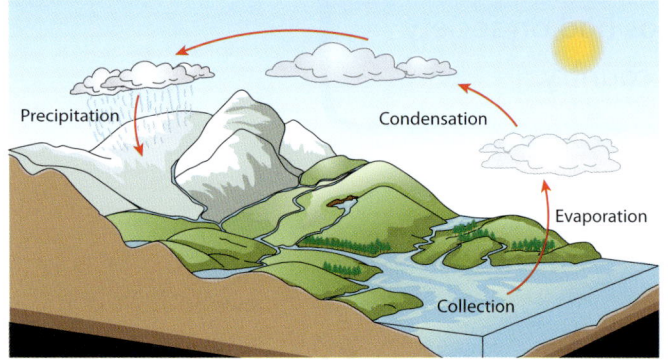

The quality of drinking water is important and millions of people around the world do not have access to safe drinking water. Human and industrial waste is routinely emptied into water sources and pollutes the supply.

▲ Many people spend many hours a day simply collecting water from natural sources such as lakes and streams.

As a country develops there are competing demands for the water that is available. A growing population needs water but also needs food. An estimated 70 percent of the world's fresh water is used in agriculture. Many other industries also use up huge amounts of water.

◀ In the water cycle, water evaporates from the Earth's surface into warm air. Air cools as it rises and the water condenses into droplets which form clouds. Moisture droplets get larger and eventually fall as precipitation.

Land

Land is a useful resource only if it can be used, for example for farming or raising animals. It needs to have characteristics such as fertility. The characteristics of a terrain affect the human activities that can take place there, such as agriculture, housing, industry, business and transport.

▲ The type of landscape sometimes determines which human activities can take place.

Vegetation and animals

The environmental conditions in any given area determine the kind of vegetation that will be found and the species of animals that will survive. As these are sources of food, their availability affects the quality of the diet and the size of population that can be supported.

Minerals and fossil fuels

Minerals and fossil fuels are distributed according to the **geology** of an area. Minerals, such as iron and diamonds, are found in greater amounts in areas that have experienced geological activity, such as the movement of **tectonic plates**. Fossil fuels, such as coal and oil, are found in places where the underlying rocks are **sedimentary**.

Activities

1. Make simple flow charts that show the consequences of having different amounts of water, land, vegetation and animals, minerals and fossil fuels. Show the consequences of having (a) a large amount (b) a little (c) none of each resource.
2. Do some research to find out the world distribution of the following resources: (a) agricultural land (b) a mineral fuel (c) a precious metal or stone.

4.3 Global issues 2

In this lesson you will learn:
- to describe the consequences of uneven global resource distribution.

Human population distribution

People have always gathered and settled in places where they could find the resources they needed. This has produced a pattern of settlement on a global scale that sees larger populations in Asia, North America and Europe than in Africa, Australia and South America. Many people no longer have to live near the resources they need because the resources can be brought to them. For this reason people are migrating further from their homeland and in greater numbers.

▲ Singapore is now one of the world's most densely populated countries.

Did you know?

China's manufacturing sector has grown very quickly and a huge amount of the goods bought around the world are made there. Of all the personal computers made in the world in 2011, China made over 90 percent, and of all the mobile phones, over 70 percent. In 2014, China was estimated to have produced 398.8 million microcomputers and almost as many smartphones.

Industrialisation

Countries that industrialised in the 19th century had the resources they needed to begin the process, such as coal, clay and metals. Soon they had the wealth to buy resources from other places. These places are called 'highly industrialised'. They are densely populated and use large amounts of the world's resources. Many developing countries such as South Africa, Mexico, Brazil, China, India, Indonesia, Malaysia, Philippines, Thailand and Turkey have reached the point where they are now industrialising. Some of these countries are now exploiting their own resources, such as coal in China and India, as well as importing resources from other places.

Economic activities

Resources create opportunities for employment in a range of industries. For example, a land that has many orange trees means that there is work for growers, harvesters, packers, drivers, shopkeepers and bankers. There is also work in factories that process oranges to make orange juice. A wide range of available resources produces job opportunities in many different areas of work. When there are limited resources, the range of economic activity is restricted and there are few benefits from the resource.

▲ In countries with limited resources the different possibilities for employment are also limited.

Economic activity and standards of living

Resources generate wealth for a country and for individuals. Both of these are necessary if the general standard of living in a country is to improve. Countries with fewer resources are less able to bring about this wealth.

Trade

One way in which countries can increase their ability to improve their economy and the standard of living of the population is to trade with other countries. This trade gives them access to the resources they need to stimulate economic activity. Countries with few resources, or resources that are of comparatively low value, will struggle to trade with resource-rich nations.

Conflicts and colonisation

The desire of certain countries to control the resources available have resulted in colonisation and periods of conflict. Even today a country may have natural resources, but not have a high standard of living for its people. Human activities, for example in the form of conflict, continue to affect the distribution and use of resources.

Activity

Work in a group to make a presentation that explains the consequences of the uneven distribution of resources around the world.

4.4 Global issues 3

In this lesson you will learn:
- to understand the concept of inequality
- to identify some examples of global inequality
- to suggest some strategies to address inequality.

Global inequality

One consequence of the unequal distribution of natural resources has been an uneven rate of development in different countries around the world. This means that the standard of living and the quality of life that people experience around the world is different.

Our 'standard of living' is usually understood to be about the degree to which we can meet our physical needs for food, water, clothing and shelter. If we have a reasonable standard of living then all of these needs can be met. As our standard of living improves we are able to have some of the things we want, rather than only the things we need.

When assessing our 'quality of life' we usually consider other aspects that are not directly about meeting physical needs. Quality of life is to do with having a healthy, safe and prosperous life. People's ability to achieve this varies greatly depending on where in the world they live.

In 2000, the United Nations produced a set of Millennium Development Goals (MDGs) which were aimed at addressing some of this global inequality.

▲ Some people, for example in remote rural parts of the world, face severe challenges as they seek to improve their quality of life.

Health inequality

There is a global inequality in terms of health. More developed countries have resources to spend on creating and maintaining high-quality health services. Most people in these countries have the benefit of good healthcare and sufficient nutritional food and safe, clean water.

Aspects of health inequality addressed in the United Nations MDGs were reducing **child mortality**, improving maternal health, combatting widespread diseases and increasing the number of people with access to clean water and good sanitation.

▲ There have been huge improvements in the levels of children attending primary school.

Prosperity

Prosperity is to do with earning enough money to meet your needs and to access other aspects of life beyond this such as education. Education is also the key to improving the chances a person has of achieving a measure of prosperity in later life. The United Nations Millennium Development Goal was to achieve universal primary education. In other words, the aim was that every child should be able to receive primary education.

Safety

Feeling safe and secure is an important part of enjoying a good quality of life. The United Nations and other organisations work towards friendly relations between countries and promoting peace around the world. Unfortunately there are many situations in the world where people have to live with the devastating consequences of conflict and war.

Activity

Find out about the progress being made in achieving the United Nations Millennium Development Goals in your country and in one other country in another part of the world.

4.5 Poverty reduction

In this lesson you will learn:
- how poverty is defined
- to identify ways in which poverty can be reduced
- about international efforts to reduce global poverty.

What is poverty?

The World Bank defines poverty in terms of whether households or individuals have enough resources or abilities to meet their immediate needs.

Defined in this way, poverty has a number of obvious consequences. Poverty means living in conditions where you do not have adequate shelter, you do not know if you will have enough food for your next meal and do not know if the food you get will provide the nutrients you need.

Poverty means living with illness or disease because you have to drink dirty water or you do not have the money to pay for medical care. It means that you cannot expect to live as long as people who are wealthier.

Poverty often means that you have little chance of getting educated because you cannot afford the fees or because your family needs you to work rather than go to school.

Poverty means more than simply a lack of money. Poverty means that you are unable to take part in many parts of society and have almost no power to change your situation.

▲ It is very difficult to escape from a situation of poverty.

Measuring poverty

The 'poverty line' is a worldwide standard which sets the minimum amount of money per day to satisfy basic needs in a given country. If a person has to live on less than this amount of money per day, then he or she is said to have fallen below the poverty line. The international poverty line today is $1.25. Just over a billion people are estimated to be in this situation of extreme poverty. Almost half of the entire population of the world – about 2 billion people – live on less than $2.50 a day.

Ending poverty

World poverty mostly affects people in developing countries, especially those in remote and rural areas. The causes of poverty are complicated and it is not an easy problem to solve. These are some measures suggested to tackle the problem:

- Governments of richer countries can offer financial aid.
- Richer countries can help poorer countries develop their economies by trading and supplying training and equipment.
- Poorer countries have often needed to borrow money. Richer countries can cancel these debts or offer special terms of repayment.
- Companies in the private sector need to invest in businesses and provide work.
- People can move to another country to work and send some of their earnings back home. These payments are called 'remittances' and are an important part of a poorer country's economy.

◀ Providing education and training for the population is a way for countries to help citizens and the country prosper.

Activity

Write a brief description of some of the results of poverty and suggest two ways that global poverty might be reduced.

4.6 International response

> **In this lesson you will learn:**
> - about some international organisations and initiatives to address global issues.

Global awareness

People living in a village have close social connections, interdependence, knowledge of everyone's wants and needs and a need to co-operate to ensure survival. As this could be true for everyone in the world as well, the world has been called a 'global village'.

Improvements in communication have created worldwide social and business networks. People in one part of the world know immediately about a situation in a distant location. This has led to a growing feeling that all humanity is connected. Individuals and communities have more insight into global issues and are more able to react to them.

There have also been scientific advances that help us understand how some of the Earth's major natural processes work, how these are connected and the effects human activity can have.

▲ Countries like Cambodia contribute the least emissions associated with climate change but are the ones that will suffer the greatest consequences.

There has also been a change in attitude towards the role of richer, more powerful nations. Rather than simply being able to have power and control, people now expect these nations to act responsibly and to assist poorer countries.

The United Nations

Perhaps the largest and best-known international organisation is the United Nations (UN). This was founded in 1945 at the end of the Second World War. It had 51 founding members, including Egypt and Saudi Arabia, and now has 193 nations. The UN has four main purposes:

- to keep peace throughout the world
- to develop friendly relations among nations
- to help nations work together to improve the lives of poor people, to conquer hunger, disease and illiteracy and to encourage respect for each other's rights and freedoms
- to be a centre for co-ordinating the actions of nations to achieve these goals.

Since there is a better understanding of how different issues are connected to one another, the UN works in many different areas, from disaster relief and refugee protection to sustainable development and environmental protection. The UN also has programmes connected with:

- health, co-ordinated by the World Health Organisation (WHO)
- education, co-ordinated by the United Nations Educational, Scientific and Cultural Organisation (UNESCO)
- the reduction of hunger, co-ordinated through the World Food Programme (WFP)
- finance, co-ordinated by the International Monetary Fund (IMF) and in partnership with the World Bank Group.

There are many other government and non-government organisations (NGOs) that operate at an international level in many areas including environmental protection, disaster relief, human rights and poverty reduction.

▲ Governments and other international agencies respond to natural disasters such as the Kashmir floods of September 2014.

Activity

Research some of the work of one international organisation and produce a poster that explains what the organisation does.

4.7 Resources

In this lesson you will learn:
- to identify ways in which individuals can respond to the global issue of using resources.

To call something 'global' sometimes makes people feel that there is little or nothing that they can do as individuals. However, there are many cases where individuals can make an important contribution.

Use of fossil fuels

Many people accept that there is a link between the emission of 'greenhouse gases' produced by burning fossil fuels and an increase in the average global temperature. The problem must be tackled at a global government level.

At the same time individuals have to look at their own lifestyles and how much of that relies on using energy from fossil fuels. The further and faster a vehicle is driven, the more fuel is used. The more cooking done using a gas cooker, the more gas is used. The links between fossil fuels and an energy such as electricity are less obvious. This is a clean and efficient form of energy in the home but is often generated in power stations using different fuels including fossil fuels such as coal or gas.

▲ Householders and businesses can install rooftop solar panels to produce electricity.

As well as cutting down on electricity use in the home, at work and at school, individuals can support the development of energy production from renewable sources, such as solar and wind power.

Consumption of other resources

People consume other resources at an alarming rate. Populations are growing in countries such as India and China and more people want to achieve a higher standard of living. This means that they will consume more resources. More energy will be needed to make the things they want to buy. Some people suggest that to allow for this, people in the richer, developed countries need to reduce their consumption of resources.

There is a growing global initiative, centred around an idea that people should 'reduce, re-use and recycle'.

As well as recycling, consumers can reduce the amount of resources they consume by making the things they have last as long as possible and by avoiding waste. Consumers should only buy what they need, especially food. In many developed countries people throw away a third of the food they buy.

▲ Large amounts of computer equipment and mobile phones are discarded because people want the latest electrical items.

Re-use initiatives encourage people to buy re-usable items such as water containers, rather than disposable plastic bottles.

Recycling aims to have materials such as plastics, cardboard and aluminium recycled from one use into another which reduces the amount of new resources that are needed.

Activities

1. List some ways in which you could reduce the amount of resources you consume.

2. Work in a group to devise a poster to encourage other people to think about their resource consumption.

4.8 Waste

In this lesson you will learn:
- to identify causes and effects of global waste production
- to identify ways in which individuals can reduce the waste they produce.

Waste and consumption

The growing problem of waste is a result of the growing level of consumption. An important reason for higher levels of consumption is the spread of a 'consumer culture'. In a consumer culture status, values and activities are based around the consumption of goods and services and people choose to buy things for reasons that go beyond meeting their basic needs.

Consumer cultures became a feature of Western Europe, America and Japan during the 20th century. The culture is spreading around the world and is growing in developing countries such as India and China.

> **Did you know?**
> The Arab Gulf Program for Development (AGFUND) is a regional organisation based in Riyadh, Saudi Arabia which was established in 1980 and has contributed support and finance to 1,466 projects in 133 developing countries.

Creating the goods and providing the services that consumers demand uses up large amounts of resources. The process also produces large amounts of waste for a number of reasons:

- many products are in special packaging
- many items are disposable
- people are encouraged to 'upgrade' to newer models and then dispose of older items
- consumers want items that are fashionable and they dispose of older items.

Waste and urbanisation

Waste from homes, offices and schools that is processed by a municipal authority, is called Municipal Solid Waste (MSW).

Urban residents produce about twice as much waste as those living in rural areas. Global estimates suggest that urban dwellers produce 1.3 billion tonnes of MSW

▲ Approximately 20 percent of the world's 'consumer class' are thought to live in India and China.

every year. This works out as approximately 1.2 kg per person per day.

Increased urbanisation around the world suggests that the problem will continue to increase.

Countries of the Arabian Gulf have seen rapid increases in their populations, rapid developments into modern economies and now have some of the highest rates of urban living in the world. They are also in the top ten for worldwide waste generation per person. Massive efforts are being made by the governments of these countries to address this issue but individuals must take some responsibility themselves.

Waste pollutes natural environments. Litter can spoil public spaces in towns and is unattractive when washed up along shorelines. Waste in the sea poses threats to wildlife such as sea birds and marine life.

Re-use, recycling and disposal

Individual consumers can:

- make sure they only put items and material that cannot be re-used or recycled out for disposal in landfill
- choose items that have limited packaging
- contact producers, manufacturers and retailers to ask them to reduce packaging
- only buy goods they need
- make goods they already own last longer.

Activity

Draw a picture strip that shows five ways in which you can cut down on the waste you produce.

▲ It is predicted that unless there are huge changes, urban dwellers will produce 2.2 billion tonnes of Municipal Solid Waste a year by 2025. This is 1.4kg per person per day.

4.9 Product life-cycles

In this lesson you will learn:
- to identify ways in which products can be created to last a long time
- how consumers can make the best use of items they purchase.

Design

The life-cycle of a product is decided before it is created. Products begin as ideas in the minds of inventors and designers. The design of a product has an important influence on its environmental impact. Product design is important because it determines the resources needed to make the product. The choice of materials is important because using cheaper materials may mean that the final object does not last as long. Design also affects the appearance of an object and this often determines how quickly or otherwise it goes 'out of fashion', regardless of how well it works. It is also wasteful to throw away a product when only one part fails. Resources will be saved and waste reduced if a product is designed so that single parts can be replaced.

Product life-cycle

The concept of a life-cycle is usually applied to living things that are born, grow older and die. We can think about products having a life-cycle as they do go through similar stages.

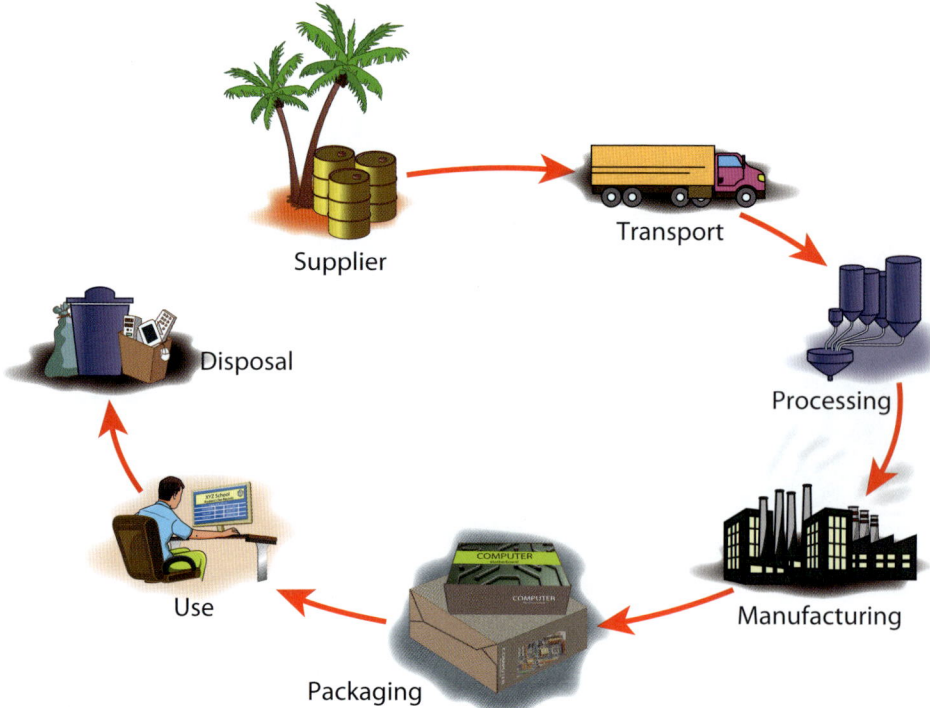

▲ The life-cycle of a product is often understood to have several stages.

Materials

All products are ultimately made from resources taken from the Earth, many of which are finite and non-renewable.

Processing and manufacturing

Processing resources to make other materials uses a lot of energy and can create large amounts of emissions and industrial waste. Making products from recycled materials slows down the rate at which new resources are extracted from the Earth.

Manufacturing is the stage at which the components of a product are put together. Clever design and manufacturing processes can improve the quality of a product.

Packaging

Most products are put inside protective packaging for transportation and for presentation to eventual consumers. Some packaging is useful because it serves to protect the product from damage, from being spoiled in some way or from being tampered with.

Useful life

A product has an intended purpose and an intended useful life. Consumers have a responsibility to use products properly and carefully, to gain the most use they can from it. Today, many people are concerned about appearances and having the latest version of a product. This means that they want to dispose of products long before they have come to the end of their useful life.

Disposal

Individuals should think carefully about the possibilities of re-using or recycling before sending an item to landfill.

Activity

Choose a popular consumer item and create a labelled diagram that explains its 'life-cycle' and how it can be made to last as long as possible. Include the responsibilities carried by designers, manufacturers and consumers to make the product last.

▲ A lot of packaging is made from material that can be recycled.

4.10 The information age

In this lesson you will learn:
- about the development of the internet and the World Wide Web
- to describe the impact of this technology on the world.

Advances in agriculture and industry changed the world in the past. What has changed the world in recent times has been new information and communications technology. These changes are centred around the creation of the internet and World Wide Web and the development of portable or 'mobile' wireless communication devices.

A brief history

Ideas about personal computers were put forward in the 1950s. By the 1960s people were working on the possibility of linking computers together to create networks. In December 1969, the Advanced Research Projects Agency (ARPA) in America successfully linked computers in four separate universities and introduced a completely new way of communicating. This 'ARPAnet' system went public in 1972 and was expanded to include international connections the following year. It would later evolve to become the internet.

Ideas such as domain names (which allow internet 'addresses' to have an ending such as .com or .gov) were introduced throughout the 1970s and 1980s. Machines were developed that could search the internet for particular information. These were the early stages of today's **search engines**.

A scientist called Tim Berners-Lee developed a special form of text coding called Hypertext Mark-up Language (HTML). This allowed for words, tables, images and sound to be displayed on computer screens. It also contained special references or **hyperlinks** that allowed people to move immediately from one page of information to another. This system of linked information pages was the foundation of the World Wide Web which was invented in 1989. This was the name given by Berners-Lee to his first **web browser**.

Through the 1990s developments continued, including improving the security of online payments. This allowed people to establish retail businesses based completely on the internet, moving away from traditional stores and shops.

Developers introduced increasing numbers of ideas for using the internet including buying and sharing music, watching video material and contacting family and friends.

◀ What would life be like without the internet?

Did you know?
In 1994 Pizza Hut became the first restaurant chain to enable people to order via the internet.

A digital divide

Access to and use of the internet is not equal in different parts of the world. Part of this inequality is due to the difficulty in creating the physical infrastructure, especially where this involves fixed wires or cables.

The internet can bring advantages to businesses and to social interaction. Inequality of access means those in the developing world are less able to enjoy these benefits.

What has made a huge difference to people in the developing world in more recent times has been the introduction of more wireless technology and satellite communications.

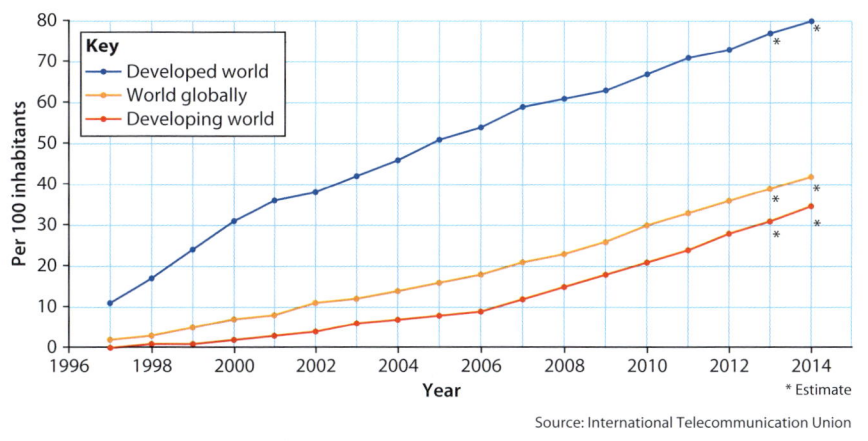

◀ Percentages of individuals using the internet, 1997–2014.

Source: International Telecommunication Union

Activity

Work in a group to discuss what the world would be like without the internet.

4.11 Mass media

In this lesson you will learn:
- to identify ways in which traditional mass media and the internet are used
- to describe important ideas concerning the contents of mass media.

Mass media and the internet

The traditional forms of mass media, such as newspapers and television, are used by organisations to communicate to large numbers or 'masses' of people.

The internet and World Wide Web give any one person, group or organisation the opportunity to do the same thing. The internet has expanded the range of people who are able to express opinions, to write and publish material to a mass audience and to try to influence public opinion. In other words, mass communication is now something that anybody can do instead of being something that only large mass media organisations could do.

Some organisations that are involved in traditional mass media do actually make use of the new technology for purposes of mass communication. For example, many newspapers have an 'online' version and television and radio programmes are widely available through the internet.

▲ A person can add some content to a video-sharing website and it can be seen by millions of people all around the world.

It is exciting that ordinary people have the opportunity to communicate. However, there is a need to be cautious about the content of any media form. People need to consider the reliability and trustworthiness of the person or organisation producing that content. With traditional forms of media, people could develop trust in publishing or broadcasting organisations. Those organisations also developed reputations which they needed to protect. The same does not necessarily apply to those who create content for a website, especially as they can remain anonymous.

▲ Readers will keep buying a newspaper if it has a reputation for being trustworthy.

Fact and opinion

An important function of mass media has always been to convey information about current affairs. The different forms of mass media have been the means by which people have known what is happening in their country and in the wider world. People expect the mass media to be reliable and to present accurate information.

The mass media also enables people to express opinions. The people expressing their opinions obviously want other people to share those views. In this way, mass media can be used to influence the views of large numbers of people.

So it has always been necessary for people accessing mass media to be able to tell the difference between fact and opinion. In addition people have to determine what reason a person or organisation might have for expressing a particular opinion.

These skills are equally important with content on the internet.

Activity

Work in a group to identify contents in newspapers and websites that offer facts and opinions on current affairs or matters of interest to the public.

4.12 Social media

In this lesson you will learn:
- about use of social media in Arab countries
- to evaluate the importance of social media in Arab societies
- to evaluate the importance of cultural values in relation to social media.

Social media

People today can create web content including text, video, photographs and other images which they can share over the internet. By exchanging and sharing this content the participants create a social network which is based online. The special websites and applications that make this possible have become known as 'social media'.

Social media has introduced a new way for people to form and develop relationships. They can be in contact with one another when they are physically separated and when they have never met in person.

▲ Many people use social media to stay in touch with friends and family.

Social media can also be used like other forms of media. It can be used to share knowledge, to spread new ideas, to share opinions and to influence the way people think about certain things.

Popular social media websites and applications include Facebook and Twitter.

Social media use in the Arab world

According to the Arab Social Media Report, there were 81,302,064 users of Facebook in the Arab world in May 2014. This represents 21 percent of the population for all the countries considered. The percentage of the population using Facebook in individual countries is much higher. The country with the highest percentage of Facebook users was Qatar, with 61 percent, while the United Arab Emirates was close behind with 58 percent.

The same report indicated that Saudi Arabia has 40 percent of all users of Twitter within the Arab world. 11 percent of the population of Kuwait have accounts on this micro-blogging site.

The impact of social media

Users of social media have what is called an 'online presence' as they are 'present' through the content they put online, such as comments and images. These are some of the advantages of their presence:

- friends and family can stay in touch and people can form 'interest groups'

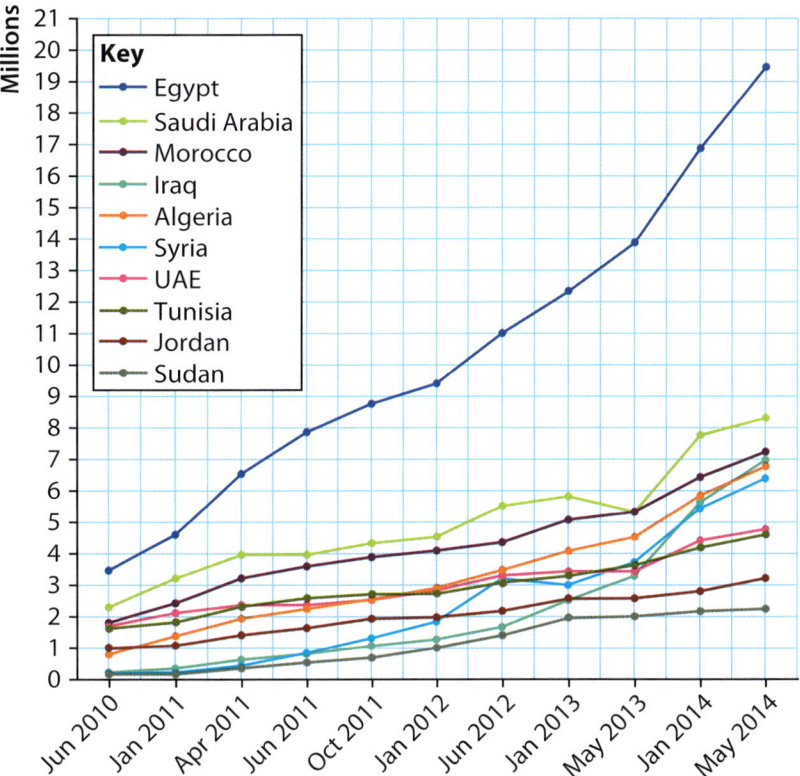

Source: 6th Arab Social Media Report

▲ This chart clearly shows the increasing popularity of social media.

- organisations such as schools can inform students and parents about future events and post recent news and photographs
- commercial organisations can advertise new products and receive customer feedback
- charities and volunteer networks are also able to benefit
- government departments can use social media to run public information campaigns and give details of their work. They can also receive feedback from citizens regarding their opinions of existing services and new proposals. This allows for governments to be more responsive to the desires of the population.

Many people believe these and similar aspects are helping to develop **civil society** and promote **social cohesion**.

Activities

1 Work in a group to research the level of social media use in your country.

2 Choose a government department. Carry out some research into how it uses the internet or social media to communicate with citizens.

4.13 International relations

In this lesson you will learn:
- to describe why national governments create and maintain relations
- to evaluate the importance of international relations.

International relations are about how modern nation-states around the world relate to one another. Many of the ideas from personal relationships, such as the need to communicate and the ability to negotiate, can be applied to the relationships made between countries.

History of international relations

International relations have developed along with the world. When travel and transport were difficult and dangerous, the connections people had with others around the world were limited.

Early contacts between groups of people from different parts of the world were often based around trade. Later developments saw relationships based on conquest and the exploitation of resources.

The complicated world we live in today means that countries are connected for many different reasons and in many different ways.

International relations today

International relations are about creating good relationships. They involve countries promoting and protecting their national interests in terms of trade and cultural identity. Relationships are maintained using diplomacy, cultural contacts, treaties and agreements.

The world today is closely interconnected and countries and people are very interdependent. As our understanding of this fact grows, then international relations become increasingly concerned with working out ways in which countries can co-operate to achieve a better future for everyone.

Unfortunately relationships can break down and this can lead to difficult times and even armed conflict.

▲ Sailors, traders and merchants were the first people involved in international relations.

Who conducts international relations?

International relations are formed and maintained by governments who are understood to be acting in the best interests of the citizens of the country they represent.

▲ Government ministers and other representatives of countries maintain international relations today.

In certain circumstances other bodies outside of governments can have an influence on international relations. For example, an environmental pressure group can influence opinion on threats to natural habitats and **biodiversity**. This can affect how governments conduct international affairs, for example banning the import of timber from unregulated logging operations.

International organisations

International organisations such as the United Nations help to bring governments together to work for global aims.

An important international organisation in the Islamic World is the Organisation of Islamic Co-operation (OIC). The OIC charter makes clear its aims which include:

- preserving and promoting the Islamic ideals of peace, compassion, tolerance, equality, justice and human dignity
- contributing to international peace and security
- contributing to understanding and dialogue between civilisations, cultures and religions
- encouraging friendly relations and good-neighbourliness, mutual respect and co-operation.

Activity

Carry out some research into the bodies in your country that are engaged in or may influence international relations.

4.14 Governments and law

In this lesson you will learn:
- to identify elements of the law and justice systems in your country
- to describe how laws are made and enforced in your country
- about some international laws.

Did you know?
One of the oldest examples of written laws is a Babylonian law-code written into clay tablets in ancient Mesopotamia in about 1750BCE. It is known as the 'Code of Hammurabi'.

Rules and laws

Rules and laws are important because they help to protect people and ensure that everyone is treated fairly and treated in the same way.

Some rules tell us the things we are allowed to do and should do. Others tell us the things we are not allowed to do and should not do. When countries have rules like these, they are called laws.

▲ A law that states that everyone has to attend school until they are a certain age means that everyone is treated fairly because they all have the same opportunity to receive an education.

Law-making: legislative and executive powers

Countries are run by governments who are responsible for making decisions about what **policies** should be followed. Governments are able to do what they need to, in order to run a country effectively, partly by using laws.

The part of government that has the power to make, alter and repeal laws is called the legislature. This is sometimes known as a parliament, a congress, an assembly or a council. In some Islamic countries it can be referred to as a *majilis*. Laws in Islamic countries are based on Sharia Law.

Another part of government has executive powers. This means they have the power to enforce the laws made by the legislature and to make sure those laws are carried out.

Most countries have a constitution. This special document sets the standards that all laws have to follow. For example, if the constitution of a country states that everyone has the right to be treated equally, then the government cannot pass a law that would mean that some people were treated differently from others.

A constitution also assigns a person or body to have the foremost authority to make decisions. One example of such a body is the Supreme Council of All the Rulers of the Emirates, in the United Arab Emirates.

Justice

Justice in a country is the responsibility of the judicial system, which includes courts and judges. The judicial system ensures that all laws are allowed by the constitution of the country and it also makes sure that all laws are applied fairly to everyone.

▲ Principles of fairness and equality guide justice and the rule of law. Why do you think the image shows balanced scales?

International law

International law differs from a national legal system because it applies to countries rather than only to individuals or single organisations. International laws work like other laws in that they are there to offer protection and to make sure that everyone is treated fairly and equally.

The United Nations operates an international justice system which is available to do such things as assist member nations to reach a settlement if they are in dispute. International laws also offer protection to people and property when they travel to different parts of the world. For example, a person's human rights apply wherever they are in the world. There are internationally agreed minimum standards concerning the way any state should treat a person from another country.

Activity

Find out about how laws are made in your country and present your findings as an information poster.

4.15 Revenue and spending

In these lessons you will learn:
- how governments around the world raise money
- how governments around the world spend this money.

Government revenue

Government revenue is the money received by government. In many countries some of this money comes from taxes.

In some countries employed people are taxed according to the money they earn. The profits made by companies are also taxed. A proportion of the price of goods and services we buy is a tax. Tax applied to imported and exported goods and services is called a duty.

Governments can also own assets, such as land, which they might choose to sell. They can also own corporations which run on a commercial basis in order to create government revenue.

If resources, such as oil, are found on government-owned lands, a private company may pay the government a concession, which gives them the right to exploit that resource. Governments also receive money from other countries when foreign businesses are established and when tourists spend money locally.

Governments also receive money from other countries when foreign businesses are established and when tourists spend money locally.

Government spending

Federal or national governments are responsible for areas such as education, health, social welfare, transportation and communications infrastructure, foreign affairs, security and defence.

▲ Governments spend significant sums of money on education.

Governments understand the importance of spending on education because this is how the members of the population gain the knowledge and develop the skills they need to take a full and active role in society. In many countries education is compulsory up to a certain age, and free. Some poorer countries struggle to provide free education and parents have to pay school fees.

Governments spend money on health because healthy people are better able to make their best contribution to society. A healthy population also puts less pressure on health services.

Governments also spend money on social and cultural development, seeking to create a happy and peaceful society.

▲ Governments sometimes offer financial support to organisations that promote social support for families and people in older age groups.

Some governments also set aside some money for 'international aid'. This money is made available to poorer or less developed countries. Governments receiving international aid can use this to assist in providing for the long-term needs of their own populations, for example by providing primary school education for all children or providing money and training to improve healthcare. Aid can also be sent when countries face a natural or humanitarian disaster.

Governments are also responsible for such things as transport and communications networks, defence, national security, law and order and developing economic sectors such as agriculture or technology.

Activity

Find out about the budget in your country and identify some planned government spending on education, health and international aid.

4.16 Democracy

In this lesson you will learn:
- to define democracy
- about different types of democracy.

Democracy

The word 'democracy' is based on two Greek words, *dêmos* which means 'people' and *krátos* which means 'rule' or 'strength'. So democracy means 'rule by the people'. The idea of democracy originated in the city-state of Athens in Ancient Greece in about 507BCE.

◀ Public discussion of current issues was an important part of political life in Ancient Greece.

Public participation

In some countries a single person or a small group of people can have all the power. The idea of democracy is that the people themselves have a say in how their country is run. People can express their support or opposition to a particular idea or set of proposals.

Even in the ancient societies where it was first introduced, it did not apply to everyone. The idea has evolved over time, and in many countries where it exists more and more people have been included in the process.

In some countries today all people over a certain age are able to **vote** for the people they think should be in government in an **election**.

In many countries there is a mixture of forms of government. A country may have a ruling monarch but there may also be other small groups of people who also have some powers. Some of the people in positions of power are elected by other people in a group sometimes called an 'electoral college'. For example, in the United Arab Emirates, individuals are elected onto the Federal National Council by an electoral college of persons appointed by the ruler of each of the emirates.

▲ In countries like India, people will wait a long time to cast their vote in an election.

Different forms of democracy

Democracy has taken a number of forms in different places and over different times. **Direct democracy** is a system that allows citizens to be directly involved in putting forward proposals and making decisions. This is not a very common system, partly because of the large numbers of people in most populations. If each person was to vote about each and every law, there would need to be a very expensive and time-consuming exercise to make sure that every person had been correctly informed about all the relevant issues before they could make an informed decision. A more common form is **representative democracy**, in which people put themselves forward to represent the people in government.

Candidates

The people who put themselves forward to be representatives of the people are called candidates. In some countries these candidates belong to a political party. The people in a political party agree on the policies they would make if their party was in government.

In some countries there are no political parties. There can still be a form of democracy which is known as non-party democracy.

Political change

Governments have to be responsive to the society of the country they govern and to the actions, ideas and opinions of other countries around the world. Governments constantly have to develop and modernise so that they keep in step with changes in society and maintain a level of mutual trust between themselves and their citizens.

Activity

Work in a group to find out about the elements of democracy in two different countries.

4.17 Citizen involvement

In this lesson you will learn:
- to identify ways in which citizens can be actively involved in society.

Local government

In most countries there is recognition that, while national or **federal governments** take decisions at one level, some forms of local government are also useful and desirable. Local government is a body that administers policies within a small geographical area, such as a town or municipality.

Some local government duties include administering or delivering the policies set by central governments. However, local governments are sometimes given powers to make decisions and to carry out certain actions. These must all still fit within the overall policies of central government.

The advantage of local government is that it is able to respond more easily to the needs of people within a given location. This is particularly important in countries where conditions and circumstances in one part of the country are very different from those in other parts, for example between rural and urban areas.

It is often easier for people to engage with and influence local government.

▲ Local governments know about special features of the landscape or of heritage that need to be protected while the area develops.

Local representatives can act as a way for the concerns of local people to be taken to central government.

Encouraging engagement

Governments need people to be involved if they are going to be able to respond to people's concerns. Many governments are making increased use of modern communications technology to inform people of decisions made at government level. These channels of communication are also available for people to make suggestions about government policies.

Governments also recognise that there is sometimes a need to focus on encouraging more involvement from certain sections of a population. For example, the Jeddah Declaration on Advancing Youth and Sports Causes in the Muslim World stated the member states' intention to 'support the development of national youth policies in such a way as to allow the youth to participate actively in formulating those policies' and 'to encourage more direct engagement activities between the youth, national leadership and senior officials on youth issues.'

In Arab societies there is a long tradition of the people having direct contact with their ruler through the *majilis*. This system can operate in small societies but as populations grow and the society becomes more complex, the system of government also needs to adapt.

Local activity

Active involvement and engagement often begins for people at a local level. It also usually involves people identifying a situation that needs to be changed or improved.

Activities

1. Work in a group to identify issues which you feel affect children and young people in particular and suggest ways they could be involved in these areas.
2. Find out about the levels of local government in your country and suggest a local issue that could be addressed by local government.

4.18 Civic engagement

In this lesson you will learn:
- to identify skills and attitudes citizens need in order to be actively involved in society.

Societies need active citizens who want to take part in society and who have the range of skills and attitudes that will make this possible and effective.

Knowledge

Active citizens have an attitude of curiosity. This makes them want to gain the knowledge they need, including aspects of history, geography and the relationships between human activities and the natural environment.

Responsible citizens want to know how economies work and how products and services are produced, distributed and consumed. They understand that societies have to make the best use of available resources, some of which are limited.

They want to understand how countries are governed and how to become involved in that process.

▲ Finding out about the history of a place is an important part of engaging with society.

Skills

Active citizens need a range of interpersonal skills, including communication skills of speaking and listening. Being able to express opinions without becoming aggressive and being able to negotiate are also useful skills when people need to reach agreements.

These skills are especially important in modern multicultural societies in which people with a different cultural heritage live together. Each culture is likely to have its own ideas, values and practices and people need to learn how to accommodate these differences without abandoning their own principles.

A range of thinking skills is also valuable. Gathering and evaluating relevant information when thinking about situations is an important part of making good decisions. Being able to consider all the possible outcomes is also essential.

Critical thinking means evaluating the available information. Creative thinking means being able to produce solutions to problems, or to see connections between different parts of an issue.

Today's citizens also often need the skills to use modern technology.

Attitudes

Active citizens want to contribute towards creating a safe, stable and peaceful society in which the wellbeing of all citizens is promoted. They will develop attitudes such as tolerance, respect and peace.

People today need to be aware of the wider world in a way they have never done before. They need to have an approach to working with others that encourages co-operation, collaboration and sharing.

They will also need to be able to deal with increasing amounts of information and be adaptable to new and fast-changing circumstances.

▲ Citizens who engage with society often have a caring and helpful attitude.

Activity

Make a checklist of the knowledge, skills and attitudes needed by an active citizen. Fill in the checklist for yourself to see how active a citizen you are.

4.19 A diverse economy

In this lesson you will learn:
- to explain why countries need to have a diverse economy
- to identify different elements of an economy.

The need for a diverse economy

Governments try to develop a diverse economy which has a range of different industries and businesses. This is sensible because if one of those industries goes through a period of difficulty, then there are other industries that will hopefully still be doing well. These industries will provide jobs and generate income. If an economy is based too much on one industry, there will be fewer other industries to keep the economy going if the main industry enters a period of difficulty.

Difficulties facing industry

Any industry can experience difficulties which can affect its **profitability** and success. It may struggle to find the workforce it needs or have difficulties obtaining supplies. Profits may be affected by rising costs of production or falling prices for the industry's product. When an industry faces these kinds of difficulties it can contract, which means it will need to employ fewer people. If the situation is very bad, the industry may close down altogether.

The economic value of products on the world market is also subject to change. If there is a high demand for a product but only a limited supply, then the price of the product is generally high. If there is a low demand for a product and a plentiful supply, then the price will be low.

▲ Coffee and similar commodities are especially vulnerable to changing world prices.

Economies of the Arabian Gulf

The countries of the Arabian Gulf have enjoyed the benefits of having plentiful resources of gas and oil. These resources have meant that there has been an adequate supply of energy as they have gone through the process of developing into the modern countries of today. There has also been a constant demand for these resources from other countries which has produced large revenues.

The governments of the Arabian Gulf countries recognise that this situation will not last forever. Even if there are proven reserves of oil and gas which could last hundreds of years, there are other factors to consider. Mineral deposits of these resources may be found in other countries which could affect the demand and therefore the price that can be obtained. The concerns about greenhouse gas emissions from burning fossil fuels are another factor that may affect the market.

For these reasons, the governments of the Arabian Gulf countries have been making efforts to diversify their economies by encouraging a wider range of businesses and industries to establish themselves in the region.

There have been improvements and modernisation in the agriculture industry and efforts to increase manufacturing. The countries have attracted businesses such as banks and companies that offer **financial services**. They are also developing a growing tourism industry.

▲ Investing in new ideas in industries, including agriculture, develops different parts of the economy.

Activity

Work in a group to make a presentation about how much your country is developing different parts of the economy.

4.20 Ethical consumers

In this lesson you will learn:
- to identify ethical issues connected with being a consumer.

Ethics and consumers

Ethics is to do with knowing what is right or wrong. An ethical decision is one that is based on an understanding of what is right or wrong and which leads to ethical action.

Ethical issues affect the decision-making process of consumers today. They are concerned about the impact on the environment of creating a product. They also want to know about the pay and conditions of workers who make or grow the products in different parts of the world.

> **Did you know?**
> Laws in Europe aim to ensure that over 80 percent of the materials used in car manufacturing can be recycled.

▲ Obtaining the resources we need always has an impact of some kind on the environment.

Ethical issues and resources

Ethical consumers want to know where the resources to make different products come from and how they are obtained. They want to be sure that the environment was not unnecessarily damaged in removing the resource, and that the process is sustainable.

Ethical issues and production

Many products today involve a complicated chain of designers, suppliers, manufacturers and retailers. Globalisation means that parts of the overall process happen in different parts of the world. Many consumer goods today are designed by people in a developed nation but actually made by someone in a developing country.

Many consumers want to know that the products they buy have been produced and made by people who are paid properly and who do not have to work in unsafe or unhealthy conditions.

▲ People are very concerned about the use of child labour.

Ethics and transportation

Many goods today travel huge distances from the places they were made to the places where they will be sold. The emissions from all of this transportation have a negative impact on the environment. Many people are trying to buy goods that are produced locally as much as this is possible.

Ethics and consuming

Another choice consumers can make is not to buy as much. Everybody has to buy things they need in order to meet their needs. Today more people are asking themselves whether they can buy a little less and keep the things they already own for longer.

Consumers can make decisions based on factors such as how far the product has travelled and if a local alternative is available. They can also look to see how much recycled material is used in the creation of a product and how easy recycling is for an existing product.

Activity

Write an article for a newspaper that explains some of the ethical aspects of buying consumer goods.

4.21 Ethical products

In this lesson you will learn:
- to identify some ethical products
- to identify factors that make a product more ethical.

Ethical standards

As consumers become more aware of some of the issues connected with the goods they are buying, there is more pressure on suppliers and manufacturers to show that their products meet certain standards. These standards are often intended to improve the social conditions of workers and to minimise the negative impact on the environment.

Food and drink

In many parts of the world, it is now possible to buy food items such as coffee, cotton, rice, tea, sugar and bananas, and other craft products as 'Fair Trade'. Producers of these goods receive a guaranteed good price and are helped to develop their communities.

The World Fair Trade Organisation is an international association with 324 member organisations spread across 70 countries.

Consumers are also encouraged to consider the effects of their choices when buying fish. The Marine Stewardship Council (MSC) is an organisation that monitors the fishing industry around

▲ Fairly traded products are usually marked with a Fairtrade logo.

the world and provides a certificate to those it recognises as operating in a sustainable way. The organisation hopes that consumers will choose to buy fish from a sustainable supply. The organisation states that its aims are to influence the world's seafood markets and to promote sustainable fishing practices.

Wood and timber products

Many people are concerned about the loss of trees and forests around the world. The Forestry Stewardship Council (FSC) is an international not-for-profit organisation which has established a system that certifies certain forests as being well managed. Products from these are marked as FSC approved and the FSC hopes

▲ Wood is used in many ways in housing and construction.

consumers will choose to buy products that are FSC-certified. The FSC aims to ensure that the world's forests are properly managed so that their future is secure.

Clothing, home and personal products

There are several ethical issues surrounding many of the clothing and household products that people buy. These include the sources for raw material such as cotton for clothing and the working conditions of the people who make the products.

A consumer's responsibility

Ethical consumerism is a subject that causes quite a lot of debate. Perhaps the important thing is that consumers realise that the choices they make when they buy products actually have consequences that affect the lives of real people in other parts of the world. It is good to purchase an 'ethical' product where this is available, but consumers still need to think about the world's environments and the development needs of some of the world's poorer nations.

Activity

Hold a class debate on the idea that people should always consider their ethical values when they are buying consumer goods.

Unit 4 Review questions

1. The process in which individuals, groups, businesses and countries around the world become increasingly interdependent is called:
   a urbanisation
   b co-operation
   c integration
   d globalisation

2. Industrialisation is a process in which:
   a craftspeople in a country use machines to produce their goods
   b a country's towns and cities are built around factories
   c increasing numbers of people in a population work in industry rather than in agriculture
   d more people in a country train to be engineers

3. Which of these actions would be most useful in saving resources?
   a Obeying the signals at pedestrian crossings
   b Giving money to charitable organisations
   c Recycling paper products
   d Showing respect to our elders

Use the bar chart above to help you answer questions 4, 5 and 6.

4. What does the chart show about the rate of population growth in Italy and Nigeria?

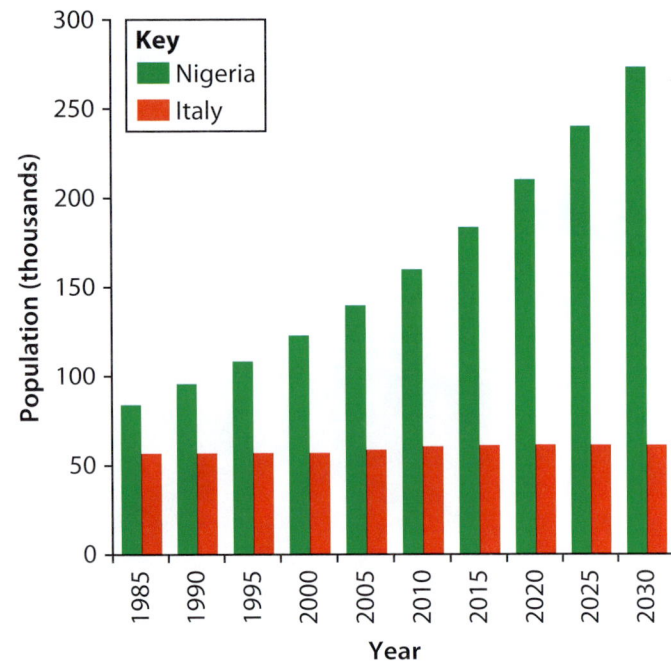

▲ Population of Nigeria and Italy, 1985–2030

5. What is predicted to happen to the size of the populations in Italy and in Nigeria after 2020?

6. What challenges might face the government in Nigeria in the future?

7. Suggest some consequences for rural areas when very many people move away.

8. Suggest some courses of action a government could take to help the poorer members of the population to improve their standard of living.

9. Describe some of the responsibilities of designers, manufacturers and users in regard to making good use of resources when consumer items are created, used and disposed of.

5 Health and wellbeing

In this unit you will learn:
- about the Human Development Index
- about the economic benefits of a healthy population
- to evaluate opportunities for improving health
- to create a useful information booklet.

? How do stay in touch with your friends and family?

globalisation   lifestyle

Human Development Index (HDI)

healthcare

5.1 Progress and development

In this lesson you will learn:
- to identify aspects of human progress
- to explain the importance of wellbeing within a society
- about the Human Development Index.

Human progress

Human societies are always changing. There have generally been improvements in people's standard of living, health and access to knowledge. Many important ideas have arisen quite recently, including the idea that we can assess our standard of living and have a right to expect it to improve.

To illustrate how recently many changes have come about it is useful to think about how things have changed in the last 200 years. At the beginning of the 1800s, some of the most developed countries in the world were Britain, France and parts of North America. People in these places suffered from many terrible illnesses which would be easily treated today. People still used candles to light rooms and workplaces and the towns had poor drainage and sanitation. Houses were heated by open coal fires and the emissions from these and from factories created very poor air quality. People's access to education and information was very limited and travel was expensive and uncomfortable. Average life expectancy in France in 1810 was 37 years.

▲ Some parts of major cities 200 years ago had very few amenities. Change has been very rapid since that time.

As countries developed, people's standard of living and quality of life started to improve. Electric lighting was introduced, more people went to school and communications improved with the introduction of a postal service and the telegraph. In developed countries today, average life expectancy is now typically 75–80 years. Home comforts have continued to improve and everyone enjoys access to education, advanced medical healthcare and improved working conditions.

There is now a belief that these improvements in people's standard of living, health and access to knowledge should be the experience of all people everywhere.

The Human Development Index

The Human Development Index (HDI) is a concept put forward by the United Nations that is based on this idea of improvement. It suggests that the successful development of a country is about much more than simply having a growing economy.

In using the HDI, the United Nations is making the link between a country's wealth and the wellbeing of its citizens. It points out that a country cannot be said to be developing successfully simply because it has a growing economy. The important thing is that the money produced in a growing economy should be spent on developing services such as education and health. Access to these is the key to people being able to experience an improved quality of life in which they are more fulfilled and can have a longer, healthier life.

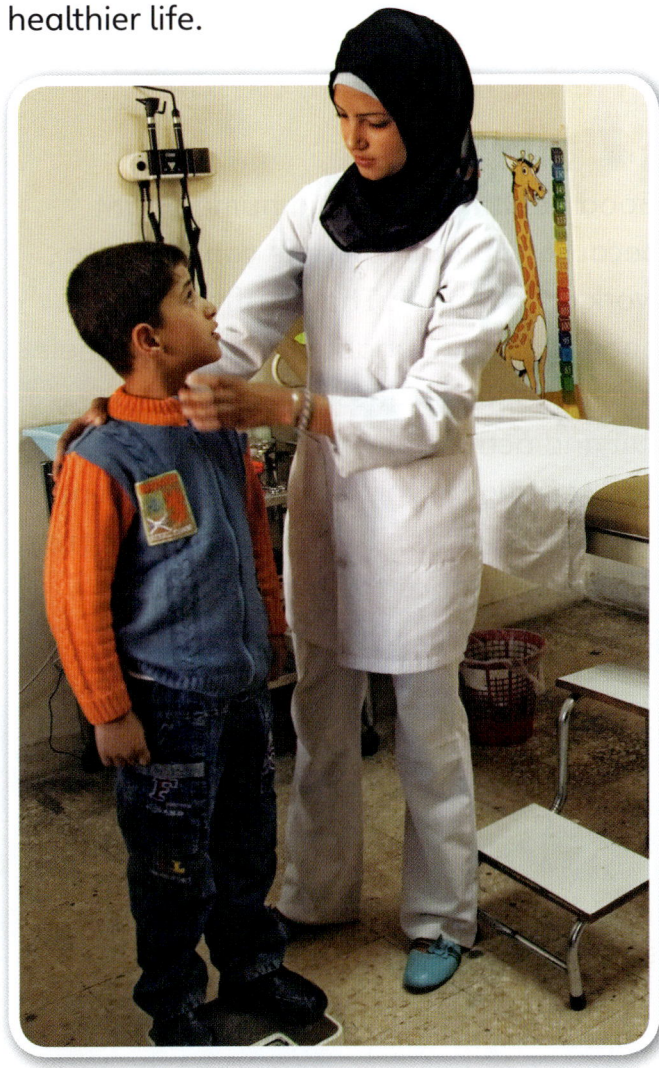

▲ Governments aim to provide adequate healthcare for their citizens.

Activity

Find out about the Human Development Index rating of three countries in different parts of the world.

5.2 A healthy population

In this lesson you will learn:
- to identify the economic benefits of a healthy population
- to identify ways in which healthy lifestyles can be promoted
- to suggest individual responsibilities regarding health
- to evaluate opportunities for improving health in your country.

The benefits of a healthy population

Good health is seen as a human right because without it people cannot go to work or to school. Those suffering from poor health are unable to attend to their family responsibilities and cannot take a full and active part in their communities and society. For this reason governments have a responsibility to create conditions that will enhance the health of the populations in their countries.

Governments also want their populations to be healthy because it is better for the country. A healthy population is more productive. Healthy people do not miss so many days of employment and they perform at a higher level when at work. A more productive workforce generates more revenue which can be used to improve health services. Healthy populations use health services less and so less money may need to be spent on these.

▲ Health is important in childhood. This is when a person's body is developing and the time for them to attend school and receive an education.

Promoting a healthy lifestyle

Governments can act in a number of ways to promote and encourage a healthy lifestyle amongst the population. They can:

- promote healthy lifestyles through public information campaigns
- pass laws that ensure foods are safe and healthy
- make sure schools and workplaces and other places where people are in groups and in close contact promote healthy practices that can limit the spread of illness
- provide places that are suitable for sports and physical exercise and create environments that make activities such as walking and cycling safer
- create economic conditions which encourage private businesses to promote fitness and health.

Organisations can:

- adopt policies that promote health, for example schools offering healthy food options
- gradually make people follow practices that prevent the spread of illness.

People need to take up practices that help avoid the spread of illness.

Health and personal responsibility

In many countries of the developing world people face serious health problems through no fault of their own. Many do not have enough good food to make them strong enough to fight off illnesses and diseases. They catch diseases because they have to drink unsafe water and because they do not have proper facilities for washing. They do not have the money for medicines to treat illnesses and sometimes the country does not have a good health service.

The major health issues facing people in modern developed societies are not to do with insufficient food or inadequate health services and medical care. Instead they are associated with a lifestyle that is characterised by not doing enough physical activity and by eating too much food, a lot of which contains too much sugar, salt and fat.

Activity

Work in a group to assess the opportunities available to young people in your locality to take part in physical activities, including walking and cycling. Make recommendations for improving the situation.

5.3 Globalisation and health

In this lesson you will learn:
- about the impact of globalisation on health issues.

Globalisation is a term used to describe how the connections between different parts of the world have multiplied and grown more complicated. This can mean that national governments have a number of challenges as they try to protect the health of the populations they govern and to promote healthy living.

Crossing borders

Globalisation has seen a huge increase in the movement of people and goods between countries. An infectious disease that begins in one part of the world can be carried across country borders and even around the world, as a result of international travel and trade.

'Convenience foods' and 'fast foods' as well as other products that are not particularly healthy are traded around the world. These foods can be marketed to make them appealing. They can also be cheap because they are made on a large scale. As a result, many people are being introduced to diets which can be high in fat, sugar and salt. Sometimes these 'unhealthy imports' replace traditional diets that are based around simple, locally grown natural ingredients which are more healthy.

▲ International trade and travel increases the risk of a disease spreading around the world.

Money and individual choice

The choices individuals make about what they eat and drink influences their health. People in middle and low-income countries may have less choice and the poorer people in these places have the least choice of all. People with the luxury of being able to choose their food do not always make the best choices.

Money, trade and healthcare

Lower-income countries are less able to provide an adequate level of healthcare for the population. Many of these countries rely on trade to earn income but the resources they have for sale are not always of high value. If the goods they trade are in competition with others in a globalised market, there may be a fall in the amount of money they earn. This means they have even less to spend on healthcare and medicines. In many of these countries people must pay for their healthcare and many simply cannot afford it.

Everyone's responsibility

Many of the decisions that affect global health are made at high levels of government. Governments of richer countries can help those in poorer countries by providing aid to develop their health systems. There have been international efforts to end certain diseases such as polio.

Individual consumers in richer countries can also make buying choices that will benefit people in poorer countries. Citizens can also support efforts made by their governments in addressing global health issues.

▲ International programmes have immunised millions of people against some terrible diseases.

Activity

The constitution of the World Health Organisation (WHO) states that 'the enjoyment of the highest attainable standard of health is one of the fundamental rights of every human being'.

Work in a group to discuss this statement and what it means for governments and individuals.

5.4 Safety on the internet

In this lesson you will learn:
- about safety on the internet.

Internet safety

The internet offers plenty of opportunities for fun and entertainment as well as giving access to a huge amount of information that can help with education and learning. There are also some dangers to be aware of associated with using the internet.

The main issues in using the internet are to do with keeping yourself and your personal information safe.

Young people and the internet

◀ Children are using the internet from an early age.

People use the internet for different things. Younger children spend most of their time while online playing educational or entertaining games or watching videos, usually on a family computer. As children get older they may have a computer of their own. They use the internet more for carrying out research to help them with school work. Some of them will use the internet to look up things such as sports results and some of them use social media sites or chatrooms.

If children have their own money, they can start to buy items over the internet.

Internet activities

When chatting online it is important not to give out personal information such as your name and address, your email address and phone number and the school you go to. The people who chat online may not be who they say they are.

Instant messaging is a way of communicating with text over the internet. Just as with other forms of 'chatting', you need to ensure that any information that might identify you is kept secret and that pictures of yourself are not included in any communications.

Some people use webcams with instant messaging applications. It is important to remember that webcam images can be captured and copied and then shared with other people.

Email is a good way of communicating but you can sometimes receive messages from people you do not know. The best thing to do with these is to delete them. It is good to remember that anything you put on email could potentially be found by another person who gets access to your account. You should never write things that might hurt or upset other people.

Internet chatrooms are special sites people can visit, often by creating a special character. It is a good idea to use a moderated site. This means it is being checked over by adults who make sure nothing unkind or horrible is being said.

When using social networking sites it is important to remember that all the information and images can be copied and printed.

▲ Shopping online is a major internet activity.

Activity

Create a booklet designed to let young people know how they can help one another to stay safe online.

5.5 Dealing with change

In this lesson you will learn:
- to identify changes people experience.

Types of change

Experiencing change is an ordinary part of life. People change as they grow older, both in terms of the way they look but also in the way they think. These are natural changes and it would be peculiar if they did not happen.

We also experience change because of alterations in our circumstances. These can sometimes affect us emotionally. For example, many people feel emotional when they move away from an area they have lived in for a long time. They feel they will miss any family and friends they are leaving behind. They may be anxious as they leave familiar surroundings and worry about what their new home will be like and how easy it will be to make new friends.

Children face a time of change when they move from one school to another. Part of the challenge here is leaving behind what is familiar and being anxious about the unfamiliarity of the new situation and about what the future holds.

▲ Moving home is a big change for everybody concerned.

Dealing with change

People can do a number of things when facing big changes. Most importantly they need to realise that the change is probably going to affect them emotionally. People need to be aware of how they are feeling about things and find a person they trust to whom they can talk. It is hoped that these people will be able to offer support through the period of change.

Different responses

People react to change differently. Some people really enjoy the idea of a change and a challenge. If people are to support one another, they need to be sensitive to how other people are feeling. What is exciting for one person may be very worrying for someone else.

Knowing yourself

Most people feel nervous or anxious about some things but feel very confident about others. Knowing these parts of yourself can help as you deal with changes. You can look for the parts of the change that you will be able to cope with well. This can help as you deal with the parts of the changes about which you feel less sure.

Know that you can handle change

It can sometimes help to look back at your life so far and to see how you have dealt with all the changes you have already experienced.

▲ No one knows what their future holds but everyone can do their best to be prepared.

Activity

Think about a big change that you are facing now or in the near future. Write about how you feel about it and about the people you think will be able to support you during that time.

Unit 5 Review questions

1. Sanitation is best described as:
   a. keeping streets and public spaces litter-free
   b. facilities and services for disposing of human waste and for maintaining cleanliness
   c. car-washing services
   d. facilities and services for maintaining the wellbeing of the population

2. Wealth, income and resources are not distributed evenly across the world. The result of this is described as:
   a. globalisation
   b. global poverty
   c. global progress
   d. global inequality

Use the chart below, and your own knowledge, to help you answer questions 3 and 4.

3. What has been the overall effect of the polio immunisation programme in India?

4. Give two years when there was a rise in the number of cases of polio on the previous year.

5. Suggest two challenges facing those seeking to immunise children in a developing country.

6. Describe some of the benefits that arise from a healthy population.

7. Describe some of the responsibilities an individual has in terms of maintaining their own health and how this can be achieved.

8. Suggest three ways in which people can act safely when using the internet and the World Wide Web.

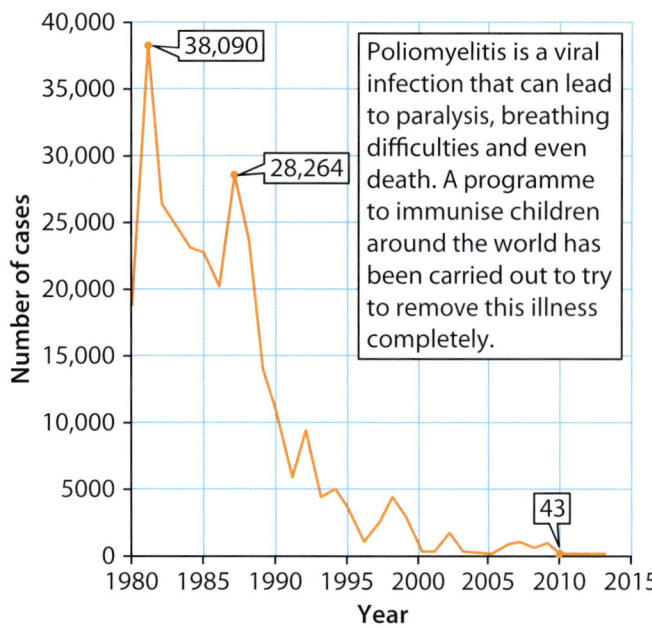

Source: World Health Organisation

▲ Cases of poliomyelitis in India, 1980–2013

Glossary

adolescence the period during which a child becomes an adult

batik a method using wax to create patterns on textiles

biodiversity the variety of plant and animal life in a particular habitat or environment

birth rate the number of births for every thousand people in a population

cash crops crops grown for selling rather than for the use by the person who grows them

child mortality the number of babies that die at or just after birth

civil society a community of citizens and organisations who share common interests and aims. Governments and businesses are not considered to be part of civil society

diplomat a person who represents his or her country in other countries

direct democracy a democracy that allows its citizens to make decisions

duty a tax paid on imported or exported goods

dynasty a series of people from the same family who rule a country

election a formal process where a person is appointed to a position based on the votes received

ethnic the people within a population who have the same national or cultural tradition

federal government a central government, usually in a country consisting of a group of individual states that have control over their own affairs

financial services economic services including banks and credit card facilities

gender whether a person is male or female

geology the origins of the rocks and land formations of a particular area

greenhouse gases gases that contribute to the rise in temperature of the Earth's atmosphere by absorbing or reflecting heat energy

habitat the place where a particular type of animal or plant is normally found

hemisphere one half of the Earth, below or above the equator

hyperlink a place in an electronic document on a computer that is linked to another electronic document by clicking a highlighted image or word

industrialisation the process during which a country develops industries

land-locked a country or area enclosed entirely by land, with no coastline

nationalise to put private land or industries under the control of the government

nationality the official status of belonging to a particular nation

norms rules that are accepted within a particular group or society

official when a language that has a special legal status is used within a government

policies a plan of action proposed by an organisation or government

population density a measurement of the number of people in a given area

production costs costs involved in the production of goods, for example raw materials and labour

profitability the ability of a business to make money or financial gain

representative democracy a democracy where elected individuals represent the people

sanitation facilities and services for disposing of human waste and for maintaining cleanliness

search engine a computer program that searches the internet for information, especially by looking for documents containing a particular word or group of words

sedimentary rock formed from sand, mud, etc. that settles at the bottom of a body of water

social cohesion the bonds that unite a society in ways that enhance the wellbeing of all members

sovereign state when a nation governs itself and is not dependent on any other power or state

standard of living the degree of wealth, material possessions, comfort and availability of services that people have

stereotype an oversimplified idea about a person or group that is widely believed

strategic connected with getting an advantage in a war or other military situation

tectonic plates the huge sections of the Earth's outer crust that move in relation to one another

terrain an area of land and its physical features

topography the physical features of an area of land

tributary state a state that makes regular payments to another country

urban area an area covered by a town or city

vote a choice that people make to indicate a preference for one person, proposal or situation over another

water cycle the process in which water evaporates from the Earth's surface, enters the atmosphere and returns to the Earth as precipitation

web browser a program for finding and presenting information on the World Wide Web

Great Clarendon Street, Oxford, OX2 6DP, United Kingdom

Oxford University Press is a department of the University of Oxford. It furthers the University's objective of excellence in research, scholarship, and education by publishing worldwide. Oxford is a registered trade mark of Oxford University Press in the UK and in certain other countries

© Pat Lunt 2015

The moral rights of the author have been asserted

First published in 2015

All rights reserved. No part of this publication may be reproduced, stored in a retrieval system, or transmitted, in any form or by any means, without the prior permission in writing of Oxford University Press, or as expressly permitted by law, by licence or under terms agreed with the appropriate reprographics rights organization. Enquiries concerning reproduction outside the scope of the above should be sent to the Rights Department, Oxford University Press, at the address above.

You must not circulate this work in any other form and you must impose this same condition on any acquirer

British Library Cataloguing in Publication Data
Data available

9780198356868

20 19 18 17 16 15 14 13

The manufacturing process conforms to the environmental regulations of the country of origin.

Printed in Great Britain by Bell and Bain Ltd., Glasgow

Acknowledgements

The publishers would like to thank the following for permissions to use their photographs:

Cover photo: Andreas Brandl/Robert Harding Photo Library, P3: Chris Mellor/Lonely Planet Images/Getty Images, P7: Jack.Q/Shutterstock, P8: Szasz-Fabian Jozsef/Shutterstock, P15: Dangubic/istock, P17: Michel Gounot/Godong/Corbis/Image Library, P18: Zvonimir Atletic / Shutterstock.com, P20: Alex Treadway/National Geographic Creative/Corbis/Image Library, P21a: xxz114/Istock, P21b: Claudio zaccherini/Shutterstock, P22: Markus Mainka / Shutterstock.com, P23: OPIS Zagreb/Shutterstock, P25a: ZUMA Press, Inc. / Alamy, P25b: Peter Adams/Corbis/Image Library, P27: Wei Fang/Moment Select/Getty Images, P29: Heritage Images/Hulton Fine Art Collection/Getty Images, P30: Aleksandar Todorovic/Shutterstock, P31: Ian Trower/JAI/Corbis, P32: Leemage/Corbis/Image Library, P33: Bertl123/Shutterstock, P36: Charles Bowman/Robert Harding World Imagery/Corbis/Image Library, P38: Leemage/Corbis/image Libray, P39: Time Life Pictures/Getty images, P40: Sylvie Van Roey/arabianEye/Corbis/Image Library, P41: Philippe Lissac/Photononstop/Getty Images, P42a: MAIKO/Shutterstock, P42b: jayjayoo7_com/Istock, P45: CORBIS/image Library, P46: CORBIS/image Library, P47: Alinari Archives/Contributor/Alinari/Getty Images, P51: Bettmann/Corbis/Image Library, P52: © Bettmann/Corbis/Image Library, P53: Corbis/Image Library, P55: Hulton-Deutsch Collection/Corbis/Image Library, P56: Paul Andrew White/Demotix/Corbis/Image Library, P57: Kami/arabianEye/Corbis/Image Library, P58: Katarina Premfors/arabianEye/Corbis/Image Library, P59: Rus S / Shutterstock.com, P61: Iain Masterton/Photographer's Choice/Getty Images, P63: Herianus/iStock, P65: Paweł Opaska/Dreamstime.com, P67: Bartosz Hadyniak/iStock, P68: Xavier Arnau/iStock, P69: Boris Stroujko/Shutterstock, P70: fotogenicstudio/Shutterstock, P72: Jason Winter/Shutterstock, P75a: Iain Masterton / Alamy, P75b: Clint McLean/Corbis/Image Library, P78: JD Dallet/arabianEye/Corbis/Image Library, P79: Sandro Vannini/Corbis/Image Library, P80: Sorbis / Shutterstock.com, P81: Jochen Tack/arabianEye/Corbis/Image Library, P85: sturti/istock, P86: Stringer Shanghai/Reuters, P87: Philip Lange / Shutterstock.com, P90: 1000 Words / Shutterstock.com, P92: Magdanatka/Shutterstock, P96: andyKRAKOVSKI/istock, P97: Adnan Abidi/Reuters, P98: FocusTechnology / Alamy, P99: Anteroxx /Dreamstime.com, P100: Yongyuan Dai/iStock, P105: Thomas Koehler/Photothek/Getty Images, P107: Celia Peterson/arabianEye/Corbis/Image Library, P112: David Taylor-Bramley/arabianEye/Corbis, P113: © Noufal Ibrahim/Xinhua Press/Corbis, P114: Jonathan Gainer/arabianEye/Corbis/Image Library, P117: ROUF BHAT/AFP/Getty Images, P118: Matej Hudovernik/Shutterstock, P122: Angel DiBilio/Shutterstock, P123: Shutterstock.com, P125: Samrat35/Dreamstime.com, P126: Realimage / Alamy, P127: Chandlerphoto/iStock, P129: Damircudic/istock, P131: Karen Kasmauski/Science Faction/Corbis/Image Library, P132: Hi Brow Arabia / Alamy Stock Photo, P134: Laborant/Shutterstock, P135: Karen Kasmauski/Science Faction/Corbis/Image Library, P136: ZouZou/Shutterstock

Illustrations by Six Red Marbles

Although we have made every effort to trace and contact all copyright holders before publication this has not been possible in all cases. If notified, the publisher will rectify any errors or omissions at the earliest opportunity.

Links to third party websites are provided by Oxford in good faith and for information only. Oxford disclaims any responsibility for the materials contained in any third party website referenced in this work.